WHERE'S SYLVIA?

THE STORY OF AN AMERICAN CHILD LOST IN NAZI GERMANY

AS TOLD TO
Linda LaMura McFadden

WHERE'S SYLVIA?

THE STORY OF AN AMERICAN CHILD LOST IN NAZI GERMANY

AS TOLD TO
Linda LaMura McFadden

ISBN: 146096652X

ISBN-13: 9781460966525

Preface

1932, the United States of America

Mama told me the story of my birth—over and over. Most mothers do that, tell their children how hard they worked to get them into this world; mine was no exception. I never got tired of hearing how hard it was for her to give me life; I often thought of that story when I was alone—and cold. I never did like being cold.

On the day I was born, it was hot—a *city* kind of hot—where the heat clings to the buildings with no regard for the promise of relief made by a setting summer sun. That September, there hadn't been a hint of the dry, crisp air of fall, and it was already the twenty-fifth. Worse, these "Dog Days" had been known to linger along the eastern seaboard until mid-October. Back then, there was a different kind of air conditioning; the windows of the Sydenham hospital had been opened to catch the occasional breezes generated by the nearby Bronx River. Huge floor fans whirred incessantly to spread the effect among the temporary patients. Bathed in their own perspiration, women in the maternity ward were about to contribute to New York's rapidly growing immigrant population. Mama had been there for two days. This was her first and only pregnancy, and her labor had gripped her with more tenacity than the heat wave.

"Come on," the doctor had insisted, "no sleeping for either of us till this is done. You can do better than that. Bear down, now, Gunda."

Mama's eyes had rolled back, their muscles too tired to focus. She was drifting away, barely listening. In spite of her reluctance, she responded to an ancient internal urge, heaved herself to her elbows and forced eight pounds of head, shoulders and feet into a brand new world.

✡ ✡ ✡

The doctor was less forceful with my father; he'd left him chain smoking in the waiting room. "Say, can I bum one of those?" His tired hands trembled reaching for a Lucky Strike. "Got a light?" His benefactor offered the lit end of his own butt.

"Thanks..." He pulled hard on the cigarette, hoping the man's name would come to him, but there had been so many new fathers. Still, the guy smoked his brand.

"Martin Rebhan. I'm a baker," Papa had volunteered.

Relieved, the doctor released a trail of smoke. That explained the profusion of white powdery matter underneath the man's fingernails "Well, you have a baby girl, Martin," he sighed apologetically, convinced as he was that most men wanted their first born to be a son. Swallowing the smoke he added, "Decent weight; over eight pounds. Got a name in mind?"

"I'm not sure. I think 'S'—something. I don't remember. My wife, she likes the movies. Maybe she told me, 'Sofia' or 'Sylvia,' after some actress. I forget." He pulled at the green package and drew out another smoke for himself lighting it from the stub already burned down close to the skin between his fingers. His only certainty was his fatigue—and he needed a beer—or something.

The doctor was unwinding. "Well, just like another woman to keep us all waiting." Picking a piece of paper from his dry bottom lip, he allowed the smoke to pour out his nostrils, closed his eyes and blew the rest toward the high tin ceiling. "Probably won't be the last time someone will wonder what was keeping her."

It wasn't.

———

Introduction

THAT DOCTOR KNEW what he was talking about. Funny, no one ever remembered *his* name, but it was true; most of my childhood was about some kind of *waiting*. Sometimes people were waiting for *me*. Mostly, I was waiting for *them*. It would have been easier to tell *how*, if *I* had remembered more, could report *exactly* what I saw and heard, but I didn't always notice details nor was I told what others were thinking at the time. I was very young when we *all* began to wait—and now my memory is fading.

What follows *is* the story of my childhood, my coming of age in the United States—and Germany, and it covers the years from 1932 until 1946. What happened to me might have been of little interest were it not for the fact that these countries started fighting one another in what was called World War Two (WWII), and I ended up in Germany in the middle of it.

My birth certificate mistakenly confirms that a "Betty Sophia Rebhan" was indeed born to Martin and Gunda Ruppenstein Rebhan at 4:00 AM—and that as a new citizen, I was registered in New York City in the county of Bronx in 1932. My mother called me, "Sylvia," as that had been her intention all along. She didn't do anything to correct the official record—she never did tell me why—everyone just went on referring to me as, "little Sylvia." Adults were like that then; more apt to tell children *what* to do and say rather than share their reasons, so of course I learned not to ask. But I always wanted to set the record straight—to at least add some of what I witnessed first hand during those noisy, harrowing, mostly lonely—but exciting times. So, I have tried to recall. It may have to be enough to assume that while many parts of my story are certifiable, it wasn't possible to present all of them precisely—and some I only learned about—later.

I still am not sure why my memories are so erratic; perhaps I thought some events were best forgotten. Yes, there were family members who might have been able to fill in the gaps, but most are dead, and considering that some of them hid darker motives, perhaps even now *they* wouldn't have wanted to say anything, or for that matter, have *me* say anything, either. So—I waited a long time to tell the story of how I got separated from my Mother during the war. It was hard on both of us. As an adult, she suffered more; she thought I was lost—and so she grieved. I knew where I was, but I had to find a way to live without her—that was my challenge. The war seemed a remote factor, until I learned to be afraid. That would come later.

I know those were troubled, horrific times; war is war. I can only ask you to believe me when I say that there were people then who spoke about it as something separate from their lives; "The war." Perhaps that is what they had to do to spare themselves from the horror of a "bigger picture," people dying; people killing one another; but even today, I haven't really been able to wrap my mind around all of the worst of it. What I do recall is the challenge of survival, what it took for me live in a place where millions died. My friends convinced me that I should share what happened to me and my family for history's sake—that it has value as a genuine story—a family in the midst of hardship, personal as well as political—and let people put it together with other pieces and judge for themselves. Some have called my living a miracle, some have chosen, "Karma" or "fate". I think I may have survived because I *didn't* always notice—e*verything.*

Essentially, the facts are these: Of my mother's two sisters, it was Aunt Betty after all who came on a visitor's visa from Germany to help take care of me when my parents bought the bakery in the Bronx. She married Walter, a naturalized citizen. In March of 1939, when only six and one-half years old, I went to Germany with them. Part of the plan was for the three of us to spend "some time" vacationing and visiting my other aunt, Agnella the nun. I was going to be introduced to my grandparents while Betty renewed her visa to accommodate her marriage. My mother and father were supposed to stay in America. He seemed anxious to have me go. My mother wasn't as certain. She let me sail away because she trusted

Betty and Walter to bring me back to New York before school started in the fall.

They didn't.

They couldn't.

———

CHAPTER ONE
The Bronx

WHEN I FIRST lived in the Bronx, I called my mama, "Mutti." What I knew about that part of New York City, I learned from her—and she was not the best at local history, but even she knew that in the mid 1930's, life in American was "touch and go." The Great Depression was pressing down to a point where it reached deep into the physical and psychic pockets of the citizenry. Thousands were still unemployed; money was tight. The rich were beginning a comeback from the loss of inflated fortunes, but the poor had nothing to divert their attention from the downward squeeze. Many years later I read that the city, regardless of its stalwart Lady Liberty lifting her welcoming lamp, remained particularly hard on its newcomers. Just north of the stock exchange where the infamous "crash," of 1929 had reduced hopes and dreams along with bank accounts, Manhattan housing was deteriorating. Landlords, already suspect as a heartless few, had insisted that they had no funds left for repairs and upkeep. European émigrés who remained certain that life would be better in the United States had to make a hard choice; some moved to another of the city's five geographical sections dubbed, "Boros." Many with Irish and Italian relatives would travel out along the area's "Long Island" to find affordable housing in Brooklyn. A conspicuous number of those of German decent moved uptown to the Bronx.

For my parents, a manageable life in a new metropolis had been dependent on many factors other than decent rentals. Because of Germany's participation in the First World War, they had been part of America's *limited* German immigration quota. Sponsored by relatives and friends, both my father and mother had promised the new government that their schooling and previous training would result in their being law abiding, productive members of the community. As *legal* "aliens," they would have all the rights and privileges afforded their neighbors who had been born there. The city suburbs offered them the cultural comforts of those who spoke their language—and English. Like others before them with practical needs, they could take advantage of the established local shops or take cheap, rapid public transportation downtown to work in Manhattan. Uptown restaurants and stores offered familiar and affordable foodstuffs; and the young, those not yet married could find local groups where they could "meet someone." In the Bronx, German Americans had access to a subway line, the Interboro Rapid Transit (IRT), the "D" train, well established churches, movie theaters, and for some, use of the Grand Concourse, properly known as the "Grand Boulevard."

First constructed in the early part of the 20th Century, the roadway was built to keep bicycles, horses and pedestrians in eleven separate lanes. While four and one-half miles long, it was meant to be an innovative invitation to travel to what would be parkland north of the city. Apartment buildings inspired by artists following the Art Deco and Art Moderne styles lined the roadway. Twenty or so blocks from the fountain at 138th Street, in a small apartment on College Avenue, Mutti and Papa began their married life.

———

CHAPTER TWO

Location, Location

WHEN THEY WERE only "Martin and Gunda," my parents actually had vague memories of knowing one another in Germany. They met again at a New York, German-speaking social club where members could dance and "hang out." My father and his young friends went regularly to drink and check out the ladies. They were, they thought, typical Bavarians, robust, healthy, fun loving—many having grown up and worked in the country's farmland. They prided themselves on their stamina, and could consume their share of beer and still go to work in the morning. The girls tended to go in groups. My father was "taken" with an exceptionally attractive eighteen-year-old. A Bavarian by birth, my mother, Gunda Ruppenstein bore little resemblance to the majority of farm girls he had left behind. Slender, stylish, with hair neatly done in a fashionable bob, she bore a remarkable likeness to the American movie star, Hedy Lamarr.

Mama always said Papa was, "smitten." Tall, lanky and glib, he was quick to ask the dark haired "looker" for a dance. He soon discovered that they had known each other, through a family connection. While he had grown up on a farm, she was the more cultured daughter of a Prussian Officer who had become a railroad stationmaster. Both had older family members in common and it seemed were second cousins. Neither considered that an impediment. Historically, European families had intermarried to protect the land, the family wealth and the lineage. While none of these factors held sway in America, the couple felt a kinship. Within months of renewing their acquaintance as young adults, they married. Within a year, they were my parents.

Mama had continued to work as a baby nurse for a Long Island doctor, but after becoming pregnant with me, she "retired." Papa, and his salary as a bakery worker, became their sole support. They moved into a one-bedroom apartment and considered their options. My mother had saved much of her income enabling them to purchase a small, but adequate bakery with a modest capacity for other food services. Situated in Harlem, near a neighborhood in the Bronx dubbed, "Coogan's Bluff," the storefront's narrow plate glass window announced the business as a "luncheonette," although its seating capacity was limited to three small tables with chairs.

Budding entrepreneurs, my parents had happened on a powerful New York business dynamic—Baseball.

At first, they probably didn't know what the impact might be. The store, in a neighborhood dotted with apartment houses where dozens of nearby families could start their day with fresh baked rolls for their morning coffee, was just down the street, half a city block, from the Polo Grounds. The "bathtub" shaped stadium, sitting between 155th and 157th streets, 8th Avenue and the Harlem River Drive, was the final and fourth version of a facility that originally had been built and named after the horse-riding, mallet-pounding sport. Expanded and refurbished, it was about to draw over 30,000 rabid baseball fans to the area to watch the newer American pastime as played by its current residents, the New York Giants. What my parents *did* know was that on occasion, "plenty" of Giants fans would walk by their store on their way to the stadium.

———

CHAPTER THREE

Fresh Baked

"YOU HAVE A great thing going for you, a gold mine, Martin—better than a life on the farm, ja?"

It was more a statement than a question. My Uncle Walter knew a good thing when he saw it, even though he had centered *his* livelihood on remaining employed by a large American manufacturing company. For more than five years, he had risen rapidly in his work place and had chosen to become an American citizen to participate fully in the anticipated economic recovery. Walter had become a member of the Ruppenstein family by marriage. When mother's visiting sister, Betty came from Germany, my mother and Walter's older brother, Bill had "fixed them up."

Walter grew up in an industrial part of Germany often considered dull by both Bavarians and Berliners. A Rhinelander, he was deemed less than remarkable by the October-Fest crowd. Western Germans had a commonly-held reputation as more withdrawn; dull, and often poor; many were employed in the myriad of factories in the area. They were called, in a derisive allusion to a food preference, "Milk-soup Germans." Walter, however, had a trade, elevating his worth beyond that of an everyday worker. He had been sponsored by his brother who had moved to the United States in the late 1920's. "Dr." Bill had established a thriving practice as owner of a personal health center featuring massage therapy. He was well known in the area as having the first practice of its kind. Mama favored this well-established and traditional method of pain relief and was a frequent client. During her treatments, one conversation led to another. When she mentioned that she had a visiting younger sister, the doctor brought up his serious minded, single, but well-employed younger brother, Walter. It was a given; soon after being introduced, the singles became a couple. They married—and moved to the Bronx.

✡ ✡ ✡

Walter had taken to stopping in after work on his own to pick up baked goods. More Mama's friend than Papa's, it wasn't unusual for him to linger for a moment while the dough was set to rise for the next day's baking. He found the process intriguing and would watch in silence as my father folded the dough into large mounds, fascinated by the quickness of the technique and the violent pounding the baker made with a flour-covered fist.

Once, Uncle Walter brought up the idea of permanence. "You must at least consider becoming citizens."

The pounding had intensified.

"Martin doesn't think like you." Mama said touching her friend's arm. "He still thinks all things are better in Germany."

"Ah, but he is here, is he not? You could take out the papers, Gunda."

"No time."

"You have to make it a priority," he smiled. "Betty and I are going to have to take care of her visa, in the near future. Her visitation years will be up when Sylvia turns seven." He ran his fingers through my soft curls. "This one will do well here, and she's so pretty." I adored him.

"She's a citizen already, "by birth, my Sylvia. She has an American certificate." Mama ignored Papa's down turned mouth.

It didn't stop Walter from asking, "What does your father think of his American granddaughter?" My Uncle knew his wife's view of life under the Prussian Major's iron rule; he hoped his question didn't offend my mother. But the independent *Gunda* spoke up without hesitation.

She put her hand under my chin. "Sylvia was an adorable baby; a butterball—and always with those curls. Strangers came to me to say how sweet she was. But I don't know that Papa is that impressed with anything of mine. He is a hard man. I am sure he never wanted me to leave the Ebrach house...

and he wasn't all that...well, did Betty tell you the circumstances of our marriage?"

"I've seen your wedding portrait."

"Oh that!" Mama shared a secret I hadn't known till then. "Yes, well, we managed to convince my father that we had been married in the church, in a proper ceremony with that photograph."

"I don't..." Walter didn't get it.

"We rented the dress and had a formal picture taken in a studio. Actually, we were married by the county clerk."

My father grinned. It was beginning to be un-characteristic. "Put one over on the old man," he explained, using one of the few American phrases he had learned, "saved a bundle!"

Mama ignored him and went on. "I went back to Germany with Sylvia because my mother was so ill. I had to visit before...well, Betty's letter was so sad. Didn't she tell you? I had to go for our mother's sake. I took Sylvia with me so mother could see us before..."

"And your father...?"

"Back at the apartment, I can show you something. I have a picture of him with Sylvia. He retired from the army but he loved wearing a uniform. You see him in a tailored, railroad station manager's jacket holding her on one arm. Both look like they are stand-ing at attention, their backs are so straight—and they are barely smiling. I think he liked the resemblance. But he never treated my mother well. He had a lady he was courting while my mother was dying. He

12

remarried within six months. Betty says his "bride" is a decent woman; *he* is still a tyrant."

"Was he the reason you left Germany? It was a very adventurous thing for you to do at seventeen..."

"I admit it. I was the rebel; but it was a good choice. Our older sister, Rosa had left, joined the convent and changed her name to become "Sister Agnella." We all wanted to get out. Right then and there I told Betty to come to me."

My father's frown deepened. He complained, "You were already planning it...when Sylvia was...what... not even one? You never said."

"We were going to need the help, Martin," Mama said, ignoring the bitterness in his outburst. "It made good sense for Betty to plan. It took time to get permission and papers. I knew she could keep Sylvia at home for us and help with the business when it was time for the child to go to school."

"Well," Walter added, "I for one am glad you thought of it." He smiled his best broad grin, lessening the tension immediately. It was his gift, one we all could appreciate. I could tell Mama liked her sister's husband. True, he was much shorter than my father, and wiry, but he had a strong face with a square chin and intense, large eyes. She told me she had found him charming when he was first courting Betty. She had often laughed at his jokes and caught herself flirting. Papa had proven less easy to please. She had chosen Martin, because he paid her a great deal of attention—and Papa knew everyone. But it was Uncle Walter who had a better sense of humor with several levels of irony. Like her sister, Betty, my mother considered him, "a catch," and he had taken to me, giving me the attention that my father appeared unable or unwilling to provide. It wasn't unusual then, for a father to leave all the child care—and caring—to the mother. Walter was full of compliments. "You were fortunate," he insisted. "Gunda is a smart business partner. My Betty is less…focused. She told me she depends on little Sylvia to make the proper transfer on the elevated shuttle train between Jerome and Anderson Avenues."

Of course I wasn't supposed to be listening to anything they said. But I remember smiling in spite of myself. It was true. Mama had schooled me at the age of four to remember how to get from our new apartment just off the Grand Concourse to the bakery, to make sure that we transferred to the right subway. Otherwise our trip would have ended up with Aunt Betty and me on the wrong train going across the river to Flushing.

———

CHAPTER FOUR

Sounds of Success

MY UNCLE WALTER had been right; the bakery business had thrived, and for other reasons than hard work and a good product—there was the benefit of location and the passion that New Yorkers shared as evidenced in their support for three professional baseball teams: My family never paid much attention to this part, but Uncle Walter knew the Dodgers belonged to the south and east—and Brooklyn. Like the Giants, they were part of the National League and were rivals for the title of "Champions." Their loyal fans adored their teams, and both "HATED" the American League Yankees who ruled across the Harlem River. Many of the men in New York baseball uniforms were famous personalities—stars. Lou Gehrig and George "Babe" Ruth were in the celestial category; their pictures were carried in and out of uniform in the much read local newspapers. Icons and celebrities in their own right, they were destined to compete for recognition through national media coverage, the radio and the newspapers. The frenzy was heightened when the two league winners played in the World Series at the end of the season that stretched from April through August.

In the late spring and summer, half of the Giants' games were played in the daytime at "home" in the Polo Grounds just "up" West 155th Street from the bakery. Some mornings when a game was scheduled, a few of the ball players and stadium workers joined the bus drivers who usually started their mornings going to the nearby store, picking up hard and sweet rolls to have with their coffee. Some baked goods, hot from the oven, never stayed in their brown paper bag.

"Can't wait." Someone had said with hot bread between his teeth.

"Better watch that figure," I heard someone say. I didn't know what a "figure" was.

"Cute kid," said a third. "What's your name?"

"Sylvia," I said with certainty. And I usually added, "This is my *Mama's* store."

✡ ✡ ✡

A few customers were more effusive than my family where children were "seen and not heard." I did my best to sit quietly in a corner, a sort of fixture at the edge of my mother's periphery. But the bakery was one of the neighborhood's creature comfort stations. There, comments on the food mingled with compliments for me. Some of the customers were also used to rubbing shoulders with team mates like Mel Ott, Roy "Tarzan" Parmelee, and the "Meal Ticket," Carl Hubbell. Others saw players on their way to pre-game batting and fielding practice. Word of mouth meant out-of-town team members might even add to the till. It was possible for some of the best known names in baseball to start their morning by putting a Rebhan roll in their mouths.

Occasionally, someone identified a ball player. "Those guys are on the team—they're Giants." What did I know? Mama was even more nonplussed. Many nights she told me she barely had time to count out the change, and wouldn't have known or cared if the great Babe Ruth himself had come across the river from Yankee Stadium and was standing in front of her. Her hands flew over the drawer of that big register. She could punch those keys and make the register bell ring, *"ka-ching,"* and push a bill into a slot and pinch out the correct change, slamming the door shut in what looked like one motion. When she got really busy, the bells would ring and ring and she wouldn't shut the drawer. She could do the math in her head. All kinds of customers came in. She welcomed everyone; grown ups, youngsters, black and white. If she didn't smile right away, and she had a *beautiful* smile, it meant she didn't have the time. She would pack up the order, and look up when she was ready to get paid. Then and only then could she return a greeting; and early in the morning, there was always someone in line.

17

A second and third baking was hurriedly prepared for the customers that followed later in the
day. Bread was put up for those passing by in the
afternoon. While it wasn't usual for lines to form
out the door, business did pick up when fans stopped
by on their way to the game, some reporting that the
smell of fresh bread carried on the wind had fueled
their hunger while they were in the stadium.

☆ ☆ ☆

It was my mother who thought up a marketing strat-
egy. Of course, she never really thought about it that
way. She just *knew*. There was nothing worse than
turning away a potential paying customer.

Some people stopped in on their way to the game.
They were carrying their "wurst" and cheese in bags.
Mother knew she would have to produce more rolls for
them to make a meal they could take in with them.
"We could get in some meats, cheeses, put up a few
sandwiches, we'll need more bread. Maybe, they'll
get their supper loaves before they get back on the
subway."

No one appreciated the Giants' business more than
Mama. She just didn't have a clue as to why baseball
commandeered such crowds. She was content to feed
a few of them on their way to a game *they* loved.

Even she had to appreciate the thousands of potential customers who plied their way past her on the way
to the World Series in the summer of 1936. I looked

that date up in a sports' book. While the fans may have grieved, the bakery business didn't suffer from the fact that the New York Yankees defeated the New York Giants, four games to two.

✿ ✿ ✿

Mama was the business woman everyone acknowledged. There were several times in the day when she was very conscious of my safety and well-being. I think she knew she was a movie star look-a-like, and that her customers liked giving her a New York once-over, but she was *busy*. When the store was crowded and I moved away from my place at one of the small tables, she would glance around with her motherly "where's-Sylvia look," and reassured, go back to work.

A modest family supper was served in the store. The grown-ups didn't sit. When we were on our way home on the elevated train, it was my Mutti who took time to put her arm around me and leave it there until we got to 176th Street. Often, Papa didn't join us on the trip home. There was dough to set for the next morning. Bedtime belonged to Mama and me. There was a story from Grimm's Fairy Tales in German, and mother's ever-busy hands were engaged in a different form of productive work. She would sit next to me while I slept; and she crocheted, making all of my clothes. Sometimes before my eyes were fully closed, I would watch, fascinated as her hands fluttered over her needle; under around and through the loops of wool. As young as I was, I knew my Mutti loved me and that I was at the center of her life, but I had to admit that she was the provider, first. Everyone's life revolved around that bakery, and my Mama was in charge of the entire family's rate of speed.

✼ ✼ ✼

When Betty arrived from Germany, there were fewer days for me to spend at the business. I knew enough to think that Mama was the prettier of the two sisters. Betty's face was solid and square; Mama's delicate and round, with a smaller nose and chin. In some ways I had missed going to the bakery; there, I could be with my mother even as I tried to stay out of the way. I had liked the slow, dark winter days best. When it was time for lunch, Mama would appear from the back with a bowl of dark soup and one of the rolls hot out of the oven. I sat at a small table and ate by myself; my parents never took the time out of their busy day, not even then. Great conversations and laughter around a table were *not* part of our lives. It wasn't what we *did*. There was none of the overt attention paid to children in today's households. While my Aunt Betty's early contributions to family life placed her in a unique position, she had found other things to do than play with me. Once she was married, she had even less to say to me.

While I was well cared for, I hadn't known enough to miss adult company at a meal. With this routine in effect, I would come to develop an attitude: You don't miss what you've never had. It was to be a life-saving lesson in self protection.

———

CHAPTER FIVE

Half Baked; the Bund

"WE DO MORE than share schnapps."

It was another of my father's understatements. He had begun to go out alone several evenings a week. Some nights he left, and then in the early morning appeared at the bakery to start his work, never having gone home. Mama said in a typical matter-of-fact conversation that far away Germany had reclaimed a native son; father was going to one of his "meetings," where German politics had become his single interest. He was going to New York meetings of the Bund.

☆ ☆ ☆

Their conversations had grown louder.

"Do you go ever up the street to the baseball?" Uncle Walter wanted to know.

"Nien. I have no desire." My father was intent.

"Harold Schumacher and Mark Koenig are on the New York team. There's a great German pitcher on the Dodgers, from Brooklyn. It's all they talk about at the factory. Who hit a home run, who steals the bases? I am learning all about it. It's very exciting."

"Humph."

"But you can hear the crowd noises when there's a hit. You can hear it, can't you?"

"I don't listen."

"But it's right up the street."

"What is baseball to me? Such a thing is a waste of time; it's stupid."

"It's just a game."

"Not a German game."

"What's the difference, Martin? The people, who go there, spend money here. You are making a better living, yes? You left Germany."

"Yes, there was nothing for me there, then."

"So?"

"Germany is on the move again."

"What are you thinking?"

"We deserve to be proud."

"Who does?"

"Germans."

"Of course we can be proud, but of what? What are you talking about?"

"The new Germany."

"Martin, my friend. Is it possible that you are just, homesick?"

"You think so? Perhaps that's it." My father fell silent.

Walter had been reading the papers. He always arrived with a folded set of pages under his arms. He knew Bund gatherings were receiving mixed reviews, some very hostile. Most of the organization's German nationalistic activities, the newly created uniforms, flags, and armbands worn at meetings appeared to be an affront to some New Yorkers. There were newspaper editors who actually titled the meetings as "Unpatriotic and Subversive." Walter wasn't sure why my father was so drawn to an organization that had blurred aims, but he learned that the man couldn't be talked out of going.

Walter read the sports section of the New York papers. Adolf Hitler, Germany's new leader, was himself doing his best to shore up political relationships. He had dispatched the boxing champion, Max Schmelling, to soothe those concerned with certain programs that he had put into effect. An athlete, with a recognizable affection for the limelight, Max had agreed to be a spokesman for his friends in high places. As to the question of problems—according to Max, there were none. He appeared to do his best to dispel and neutralize the publicity generated by gatherings of supporters of the NEW Germany in the New York Bund. As recipients of bad publicity, they were officially unwelcome. Soon enough, major Bund leaders were repudiated in Germany, and Martin and his new friends' meetings were being attacked regularly on several fronts.

My mother didn't know what to think—or even if she should bother to protest. Walter didn't know what to think, either. Perhaps his connection to my mother assured him in his belief that there was nothing subversive or dangerous in my father's nature. He preferred to believe rather that Papa was still suffering from a certain, self-driven humiliation suffered from being on a losing team, an unsophisticated supporter of "things" German. It was hard to believe otherwise. Walter came to regret not having dissuaded him. Instead, he had offered my father some personal advice.

"You work too hard. You should take the afternoon off. Go to the baseball." Aunt Betty told me that Walter had said Papa's reaction was to pound harder on the dough, surrounding Walter with clouds of flour in response.

☆ ☆ ☆

In the meantime, the Giants and the Polo Grounds were doing their best to keep the neighborhood shops in business. Once again, they won the championship in their league and played the New York Yankees in a World Series held in Yankee Stadium and the Polo Grounds. Unfortunately, the results were less favorable; the Yankees beat them again; four games to one.

CHAPTER SIX

The Beginning of "Big Time" Remembering

FOR ME, SIX was a magical number—I would be going to school. I was more than ready, and everyone knew it. We had moved to another, larger apartment off the Grand Concourse. The school was within walking distance, and having learned the route on a trip to have my required immunizations, I was anxious to show my independence and skip down 175th Street to the local public institution on my own.

A free education for all citizens had been guaranteed by the American federal, state and city governments, and Mama was going to make sure I would participate. I had watched others carrying their lunch in tin pails or lunch boxes swinging in cadence to the sound of new leather, high-top shoes slapping the pavement. Certainly my clothes were new; my hair had been trimmed to enhance its curly nature. There would be more of everything—books and stories like the ones my mother had read to me, tales of ancient people, mystical animals—and there would be children, other children to play with. I could barely contain myself.

My early school days were a blur. Mostly I remember getting the shots. The primary vaccine was scratched into my arm (I still have a big dent and scar) to resist the scourge of Small Pox; some pains are etched deeper than daily joys. My afternoons were spent in Aunt Betty's care. She was at the apartment in the afternoon to receive me and oversee homework and indoor play. In this role, Betty was more serious than she had been during our trips to the bakery in the summer. Before her marriage, she had shared a bedroom with me, but unlike Mama, she was untrained in the principles of child rearing; she had a tendency to raise her voice when asking a question or providing direction. She yelled—a lot! While I had really liked having my aunt's company, when I had a chance to be alone, I always knew I could retreat to the fire escape platform just outside my bedroom window.

I covered the strips of metal with a blanket and my bed pillow, creating my own version of a 'treehouse' playroom high above the city streets. There, I could raise my own family of dolls, feeding one with a tiny bottle, changing its wet diaper and cooing and talking in sweet tones. Life was manageable. I had my "babies."

☆ ☆ ☆

The New York City public school system worked its own way.

"We speak only English in this school, Miss."

Everyone had noticed. No matter what name my classmates would learn to print in upright letters, they would all be told to speak or try to speak in English. For the most part, I already knew some of the language having picked up phrases in the bakery. In what proved to be a short period of time, I had learned to recite and was being taught to write my name—and I already spoke whole sentences in English. My rare, sudden slips into German came from my home life. Mutti and Aunt Betty would chatter away in their native tongue and occasionally toss in a recently learned English phrase. One or the other would turn to ask, and I would fill them in on pronunciation or a simple definition. I enjoyed my position of power. Being bilingual meant the adults couldn't keep a secret—I could.

AND I knew my numbers.

"A dollar," was a more likely answer for me when my classmates had counted up to ninety-nine and were asked, "What's next?" The item missing in this new environment of mine was the "ka-ching" of the register bell. I could make change for a five dollar bill. I could jump rope held by two end-turners or skip with a rope held and turned on my own. I played tag, Hide 'n Seek and Sardines. Lithe and small I could squeeze into the smallest of spaces. Hard to find, I gained popularity by hiding until the very last to sneak past whoever was "it," freeing all those caught before me with a rallying cry of, "in free." Some days I was content just to watch the boys playing in the street. There were always several of them who carried a bag full of marbles while others toted bottle caps, which they advanced from chalk drawn bases, using their middle finger and thumb to scoot the cap forward along the curb.

There had been one certainty in my early memories. On my way to school, I had seen a doll carriage in a toy store window. I surrendered my fondness for the classroom blocks, dolls and miniature wooden kitchen shelves and lobbied for a wooden "coach" with springs and a folding hood. America was the land of plenty. I had hopes of my own.

I thought I had hoped for *it*, "forever." But my practical mother had not complied with my frequent requests. Rather, she had carefully presented September birthday wrappings holding a collection of new clothes and supplies for the start of classes. There might have been several pencils and a packet of multi-colored pads with pages glued together at the top with thin, winding string. My *big* present was a leather bound autograph book with a lock and key. The first two pages had spaces for my parents' signatures; the second, a picture of an American flag and the Pledge of Allegiance; the third, pictures of Abraham Lincoln and George Washington. It was so—American. Still, my father had signed his name and written in, "Heil Hitler."

I had tried to be grateful for all my birthday presents, but I had believed as strongly as I had hoped—still, no carriage.

✺ ✺ ✺

The pram appeared close to the Christmas tree, and next to a conspicuous pile of boxes wrapped in tissue and paper, tied with big bows and cards claiming me as their rightful owners. There it was—almost big enough for a human newborn. I was the doll-mother who had chosen immediately which of my "babies," would have the honor of being carried along in such finery. It was almost difficult to empty my stocking filled with fruit and chocolates before opening all the other gifts so that I might focus on such a remarkable present. At that point, I had everything I ever wanted.

———

CHAPTER SEVEN

Merry Christmas and Other Surprises

DINNER HAD BEEN a remarkable feast, featuring mother's regional beef goulash over steaming egg noodles, the desserts, fruit-filled Stollen, and a circular Kuchen, glazed to perfection. In a moment of wildness, I had scraped my index finger at the edge of the confection and licked all the evidence off before I could be accused of such thievery. I'd managed to get away with it while everyone was looking at Walter when he stood to announce, "I am taking my wife back to Germany in style." He moved to pull Aunt Betty up to his side.

Papa emptied his beer glass.

"We have to take care of her visa, and I want to introduce her to my family."

I have to admit, I was preoccupied—I used the pause in the meal to slip from the table to reexamine the doll carriage and its leather springs above thick, rubber-ringed wheels with chromium spokes.

Papa reached across the table for the beer pitcher and poured himself another drink.

Uncle Walter took a postcard from his inner pocket. "I've made reservations on the Bremen."

My father raised his glass. "You see. Even Walter knows the best ocean liner. It's the winner of the "Blue Riband"—the world's fastest. She will cross in less than five days. AND she is German built!"

My mother seemed breathless. "I knew you would have to go back, but…"

"We didn't want to disappoint you." It was Aunt Betty who reached out to touch Mama's arm. "You've been so good to me, but we've waited as long as we could, and we must go or lose the possibility of return-ing with a permanent visa."

I looked up from the carriage brake mechanism. Betty's voice was unusually soft when she said, "I'll… we'll miss you."

"We'll miss you, too," said Mama looking across the table at Papa. His mouth was moving without sound. I couldn't hear. Maybe he didn't want anyone to know what secrets rumbled through his mind. Mama, on the other hand, was prone to think out loud. She had lots to say even as she protested. "I don't know what to say. The business is so good—we are selling, selling, selling…three times over with the holidays—and spring is—yes spring is baseball." Papa was pouring himself another beer. She went on.

"What will we do without you? And —Sylvia would have to be left alone after school." She looked at me. "Come back and sit at the table, Snukie." It was her term of endearment. She didn't use it often but still, I hesitated, reluctant to leave my gift.

"Yes, well, we have a solution," Walter interrupted. "We have a proposal for you. Sylvia has completed half of her Kindergarten. We can take her with us—show her off to my parents with my Betty in the Rhineland, then go east and on to the farm, to introduce her to your parents, too, Martin."

Mama smiled. "Such a thing could be possible. Did you think of taking her to visit Agnella at the convent? Our sister would welcome you...and Papa; you could take her to see our father."

Mine was on his feet. "Yes, yes," he was shouting with an unfamiliar exuberance. "She can see our country, see how beautiful!" He raised his glass in salute. "You must take her with you. It is the best idea. You must!" He made his way around the table to pump his brother-in-law's hand.

He had his reasons. His mind was racing forward. In two months he would pull out his new brown shirt and arm band with its swastika and declare himself a member of the New Order in a major Bund meeting in February, 1939—in Madison Square Garden.

No one else at that Christmas dinner knew what my father was really thinking or what he was going to do. Perhaps he was reacting to his growing disinterest in his relationship with my mother. Even she knew they had gone their separate ways, customarily, he to his male pursuits, and she to motherhood and work. Perhaps, what he did consider was that his daughter would soon be in Germany—and so might he—and there would be nothing anyone would do about it. Planned or unplanned, what happened as a result would, however, affect everyone at that table for years to come.

It was done. Betty and Walter would make the trip, and take me with them. No one asked if *I* wanted to go. If they had, I might have told them that I was thrilled with the prospect of "riding" on one of those big ships. I already had a built-in sense of intrigue when looking at those that made their way into New York's Upper Bay. Of course, I had no concept of how long that "ride" might be.

———

CHAPTER EIGHT

On the Move

THE WEST SIDE dock terminal area throbbed with activity. Lines of varying length alternated between people surging forward and coming to abrupt stops. The mid-March winds had an effect on the bodies in the crowd. More than once, I pressed my cold nose against Uncle Walter's winter coat. I grabbed one fistful of wool as a handle to avoid toppling backwards. I had stopped feeling any pain in my other hand firmly gripped by Mama who had pulled it through the muff hanging around my neck. My view was of legs and torsos, my breath limited to the smells of the wharf beyond the concrete apron. The dock itself was covered in wide planks of wood that smelled like the inside of pickle jars. They were ribbed by the wear and tear of thousands of feet having gone before mine.

"Look!" Walter had lifted me above his shoulders and directed my eyes upward at the hull of the great ship in the slip. But it was not the sleek metal rising from the equally black water that had captivated my attention. I had looked back and scanned the carts loaded with baggage for one reason. I saw it resting high atop a man-made mountain of sea-going trunks, bags and parcels. I would have claimed it anywhere. There it was with its spokes, rubber wheels spinning freely in the air, the polished wood side etched with curling lines deeply carved around the edges, the center medallion winking back its mark of distinction, the familiar glistening handle. Was it possible? Was it missing its hood? No, someone had folded it down, and it looked as though it was swallowed in the morning light pushing through the terminal's high windows. I was reassured by a metal hinge sporting a large cardboard, green tag before Walter put me down.

"Look at this then," he directed my attention to the pile of cardboard tickets he held carefully in the swirling air. He winked. He offered his collection stamped, *"Cabin Luggage."* My doll carriage was sailing to Germany; it would be placed indoors, in our cabin. It would share the limited space already selected to house Betty's American wardrobe, Walter's suit and shirts and my crocheted outfits. Oh Mutti, my dear Mama had done my packing. She had seen to it. My new carriage would sail along with me.

✫ ✫ ✫

The Bremen hummed at the ready, its four turbine engines of 25,000 horsepower each chomping at the bit. Pride of the Norddeutscher Lloyd service, she had been joined by her sister ship, the Europa and they had taken turns as masters of the crossing record having only recently lost the honor to the French liner, Normandie. She was a popular, safe rival for the British Cunard liners. The loss of their Titanic had provided a new set of priorities. The Bremen carried 800 more lifeboat seats than needed for her 3,848 passengers and crew.

Mama and Aunt Betty were photographed on deck wearing identical heavy, fur coats, Mama's hat pointed at a rakish angle and Betty's supporting eight pheasant feathers that were stabbed through the felt crown setting. At the forefront of the picture, me, "little Sylvia" dressed in matching coat, hat and leggings, carefully, if hastily, crocheted by Mama's flying needles, the front double breasted panel held in place by sixteen buttons. I am holding a bouquet of a half dozen rose buds, the balance was in a corsage worn by my mother. They were Walter's gift. Papa was not there to see us off.

"Be good." Mama bent down to gather me up. "Be sure to listen to your Aunt Betty, and don't make any trouble…"

"Yes, yes, yes," the acceptable answers to directions and admonitions. I was more inclined to respond to Uncle Walter's words.

"Smile. This is the beginning of a great adventure, ladies."

My thoughts drifted away from the dock and my mother. I wondered how long I should have to stand at the rail waving my handkerchief at those remaining on land. There were my dolls, my carriage to promenade, they were sitting still for me and there would be so little time to play.

"See you soon..."

✳ ✳ ✳

For four days, my on-board life waited until Walter had brought tea to the cabin for the motion-challenged Betty. Even he had a mild case of sea sickness. With my aunt settled back into her bed with medicine provided by the ship's doctor, Walter and I would take my doll family around the upper Promenade Deck, past the two giant stacks, around the spoon-shaped stern, and forward.

I wasn't that interested in my surroundings. At least what I remember was the thrill of pushing that carriage, the feel of the handle, the smoothness of its forward motion. I barely recall the people, the fashion of the day, never mind the small plane and its catapult fashioned to launch the mail in advance of the ship's docking in a harbor. I can tell you it wouldn't be the only time I traveled *with* an airplane rather than in it. I didn't really look it over then. I was busy.

✳ ✳ ✳

The first evening, I sat with one other twosome at a circular table for ten. The adults' dinners were put down by steady legged waiters who cleared most dishes with food virtually uneaten.

"Come to us when you have finished," Uncle Walter had said to me while leading a *green* Aunt Betty away. The waiters soon knew to deliver the sea-sick passengers' ice cream to the young girl with the cast-iron stomach—me.

✻ ✻ ✻

Hamburg appeared on the horizon soon after the fourth day of our crossing. The taller buildings of city sliced their way through a considerably gray, German sky. I was surprised and somewhat disappointed; my father had assured me that *his* Germany would sparkle and wink to welcome me.

Uncle Walter had sighed at the sight of the shoreline. "We must end our walks, liebchen. Come along and we will take one more turn on deck."

It was just a city after all—and not as big as New York. Then too, it signaled the end of my little-girlish joy. I would have to give up my pram walks so that its permission-to-travel baggage claim might sit back under the pile of Uncle Walter's tickets.

Aunt Betty had lain on her bed all morning, her worsening moans rising and falling with each surge of the sea. Uncle Walter tried to assure her that the motion was coming to an end. He apologized to me as there could be no companion to stand at the rail and watch the ship ease itself into the mouth of the harbor. I would have to sit quietly inside while others watched the great ship slide into its berth. I tried to listen to the sounds of the thrashing engines and change my doll's outfit—anything to drown out the sounds of Aunt Betty's dismay.

✼ ✼ ✼

Easing myself down the gang plank to step on the concrete dock had been an unexpected challenge. Moving *while* moving had been easier than not. Other passengers commented on their own wobbling. Surprisingly, Aunt Betty walked straight forward with conviction and purpose.

"Thank you, God," Betty intoned on the stable dock, lifting her head and unwrapping Walter's arm from under hers. "All I ask is that you let me stay still for a bit," she said softly. "Go, see to the luggage. Sylvia and I will wait right here. Take your time. Please take your time."

She had found a small ledge against a wall where we could sit. Holding my hand in her lap, she closed her eyes. I saw him return. He signaled me to stay where I was while he gave the man with the luggage extra money to wait at a distance. Walter used one hand to put a finger to his lips and another to point to the doll carriage on the cart with my trunk. Not until the last passenger and crew members had filed past us all, did he approach Betty to say, "We have to go now. We don't want to miss our train."

The New York subway system had been my domain, but I was not prepared for the complexity of the Hamburg station. This time, Aunt Betty, having recovered her land legs, seemed uniquely qualified to lead us across the wide marble floor toward one of dozens of numbered tracks. Uncle Walter, once again guardian of possessions had stood in line to purchase tickets and engage the uniformed baggage handler with a cart.

"Look at all the trainmen over there." I pointed out.

Aunt Betty had turned to see what was keeping her husband. "No dear, those are not railroading workers; they're soldiers."

"But they are carrying luggage," I argued.

"Those are back packs," Aunt Betty corrected. "Soldiers are carrying their own."

"They're going east," Uncle Walter added having hurried to reach us before we had chosen a numbered gate. "I don't ever remember having seen as many soldiers in one place—certainly not in Hamburg."

"Are they going on our train?" I asked.

Aunt Betty knew better. After all, her Papa had retired from the Army and been a railroad station master for years. He never tired of telling any of his children what he knew about the mainstay of German transportation. "They'll have their own troop trains," she called back. "Don't dawdle, Sylvia. Here's our gate—and the train's in."

The tracks were already occupied by a lengthy series of multi-colored railroad cars, some of which had dozens of doors open to the platform. Large trunks were being slid up a ramp into a baggage car, while human passengers formed lines to climb metal steps. Aunt Betty was in her element. "See how the cars are hooked together? Later, in other stations on the way south, they will be unhooked and reconnected to those going east and west. German railroad tracks are the country's highways. You won't see anywhere near the number of automobiles they have in America. Papa knows how many miles of tracks there are. You can ask him. It will make him happy if you do."

Our small hand luggage went above us in racks edged with netting.

"Put your doll up with my bag," Betty had commanded. "We won't have to leave our railcar; it will leave one train behind and be attached to another. Later, we will actually change trains."

Some passengers vacated their seats when they reached their stop; others remained occupants of the two rows of bench-like seats. Aunt Betty had claimed the window seat with a short explanation about needing it for air. I had to sit upright between my aunt and uncle leaving room for a third and fourth adult on the upholstered bench. I had looked at Uncle Walter, thinking to protest at being squeezed, but he had signaled in the silent language we were beginning to develop, our ears having already attuned themselves to the rise in Aunt Betty's pitch.

The car itself was divided into compartments with sliding doors allowing for access to the aisle on the opposite side of the train. I became pre-occupied with the size and shapes of people filling in the space opposite me. Most had chosen to keep their coats on; it was so cold in the car. One woman's heavy arms seemed to rise and fall on her huge stomach. She didn't have any lap for her food. To Uncle Walter's right, a pair was sharing a big yellow onion. One man had begun to snore and his nostrils and lips moved to produce more sound than I had ever heard. I worried that my doll carriage was being equally pressed into a small space, and in spite of being folded in half, I went to sleep.

I woke with a pressing need. Easing myself from between my sleeping relatives, I managed to find a bathroom at the end of the car. Relieved, I tried to go back. My modest space on the seat had filled in, and legs belonging to the unformed-lap lady barred my entrance. The people next to Walter stirred momentarily and in a moment of unique clarity, I called out.

"Uncle, I am afraid I will disturb Aunt Betty and she might throw up again."

The onion eaters rose, pulled down their remaining belongings, and silently moved to another compartment leaving me to climb onto their vacated place. Uncle Walter smiled as I put my head in his lap. I slept lying down for one hundred miles.

✻ ✻ ✻

"We're here!" Betty was excited.

I wasn't as sure. To me, it looked like we'd taken the wrong train to Flushing.

———

CHAPTER NINE

The Rhineland

TÖNISHEIDE WAS WELL east of the big manufac-turing complexes in Essen, but it shared the look of industrial towns that dotted the area where factories employed the local citizenry in the production of hard goods. Certainly, there was nothing "quaint" about it. Walter's parents lived in a modest house on a quiet street off an avenue with a trolley line. They were friendly and open; Aunt Betty was not. She was barely able to shake hands.

"Mind your manners, miss." I was staring, so she managed to shift the attention to me. I do remember that the Eigens were pleasant, even though I have come to believe most adults at the time were not that taken with children. My Uncle Walter's easy smile was returned when he introduced me. It was, however, the beginning of my genuine awareness of my Aunt Betty's power. She was relentless with my uncle. He did what she wanted him to do—or else.

The adults sat together in a small front room of the modest house motionless enough to have had their portraits made—but no one took a picture.

"May I take my dolly for a walk?" I had hoped for some sidewalk time in the Töinesheide city neighborhood.

"We won't be staying long enough to unpack," Betty had whispered. Still, the visitors had spent several nights while I was camped on a couch in the living room. Dinners were modest; the Eigen's actually served the famous soup my father had suggested might be the main course. In addition, there was jelly on the table, which the senior Eigens plopped in large amounts on the surface of the milk circles in their bowls. As much as I loved jelly, I could not EVER appreciate the combination of something that sweet—and putting it in soup—Jelly? Ugh! I thought, no wonder people talked about Rhinelanders.

There were other relatives to see. While the eldest brother Bill, the health club founder had been in the United States for years, several of Uncle Walter's relatives had remained in Germany and lived nearby. One brother, a postman, had a school-aged son named, Werner, but those visits were not as memorable as the jelly, and while there may have been some lively conversation among the adults and other visitors, none of it had been directed toward me.

I tried to keep myself busy examining the great box cages of huge rabbits kept in the back yard. Dozens of twitching noses below big black eyes were

48

calling out to me from behind wooden slats. I just knew they wanted my attention. I fed them bits of grass and then when I tired of poking sticks into the cages and watching the rabbits chew them into sawdust, I turned to an intriguing set of their crawling neighbors, and found myself disrupting great mounds of earth, housing an unknown variety of bugs. For hours on my own, I squatted on my haunches while I pinched and poked those bugs into oblivion.

In the evening, Aunt Betty lobbied for release; twice she had put me to sleep in my clothes. Early one morning, without much notice we were climbing aboard another train.

Aunt Betty was more than quiet. She *had* been sick again and I had a seat for myself giving my uncle the job of sitting next to his wife while trying to remain motionless. The morning meal on board the train was a bit of cheese and a sweet roll, which Walter had purchased for us in the train station.

"You will be a butterball again," Walter had teased handing me his wife's roll. I ate both confections knowing full well that they weren't as good as my mother's.

✲ ✲ ✲

Gray, boxy buildings gave way to blurs of green, and smokestacks disappeared behind them. Content that my stomach was superior and full, I drifted off, waking to follow behind the luggage as it was moved from train to train. I had formed my own opinion of traveling. I didn't press my face against the window, nor was I really interested in seeing the countryside. Wherever we were going, we would get there faster if I didn't take any notice along the way.

———

CHAPTER TEN

Bavaria

THE BAMBERG STATIONHOUSE had recently had its trim painted a bright green that glistened in a welcoming sun.

"Are we still in Germany?" I wanted to know.

"Silly child," Aunt Betty responded with her patent ill humor.

"Of course we are." My uncle winked. "Your mother said this was the part of the country where children could play outdoors and get some color in their cheeks. We change trains here for one to Ebrach. There we will get your pram and your babies and take them for a walk in the sun."

And walking became the way of it. Soon enough the smaller cases and even the larger pieces of luggage were piled across the sides of my carriage and my dolls had to share the trip from the station to my grandfather's house. We stopped once for Aunt Betty to catch her breath, and the short distance was accomplished. The spring's lengthening day at least meant we wouldn't be traveling in the dark.

"There!" Betty sounded relieved. "The house is just down this street. Can you see it...the one with the woman standing on the front step? That's Papa's new wife. I wonder if she will recognize me. Oh Walter, do you think Papa will be glad to see me?"

Preoccupied with pushing the carriage, I stopped paying attention. The pace had picked up and I was pushing the carriage and the luggage by myself. Uncle Walter moved forward keeping up with, and trying to reassure, his wife. I think I only hoped we would be in time for dinner.

✧ ✧ ✧

"So, your Mama is too busy to come to visit her father?" He withdrew a pouch from a breast pocket, pinched some tobacco from it and loaded his pipe before anyone spoke.

"Papa, let the child eat in peace. You have your daughter, Betty, at your table," the new wife insisted.

"Yes, Papa, I am here with my darling Walter. We have come this long way to see you. Be happy."

"And Sylvia, isn't she beautiful?" Walter was quick to add. "She has brought her family with her." He winked.

"But not Gunda," The older man made a noise in the back of his throat.

Betty lowered her eyes and then with renewed vigor announced, "I am going to have a child, Papa." As an afterthought she added, "Walter and I are going to give you another grandchild. Perhaps this one will be a boy."

I stopped listening again. I was getting good at that.

I had my own bed. The tightly packed, straw mattress was without a sheet, the blanket, a deep orange-red cover was filled with soft down feathers that folded around my entire body. It was my introduction to a luxury not provided in my American home. Warm and quiet, I encouraged my tired legs to suspend themselves in feathers until they floated away. "Mutti," I said very quietly sinking into my nest, "I may not be the only one who wishes you were here."

My days were filled with modest attempts to help Grosfater's "new wife" (that's what Betty always called her. I am not sure I ever heard her given name). I was allowed to hang the laundry on long rope lines in the yard, having stirred the wash in a tub of water that was actually heated over a fire. Playing with my dolls appeared to be out of the question. While I remember posing for pictures with a smile on my face, I got the distinct impression that the new Mrs. Ruppenstein saw us as added work, a burden on her time and energy. And my Grandfather, well, he was Prussian to the core. I didn't like him. It wasn't a place I would ever come to love.

✧ ✧ ✧

Uncle Walter's attempts to meet with officials who could get Aunt Betty's visa to accommodate her change of status, hit a snag. He described his day at the Ruppenstein table.

"Impossible, just impossible. We will have to file requests in three places and wait for approval in each instance. It's true," Walter added trying with less impatience, "There is no end to the paper work. What I thought we could do in person won't necessarily speed up the process. But the ministers were most concerned with the Polish question."

"You needn't worry, Papa, we won't be staying here much longer."

Betty had my attention again.

"We are going to go out to Trundtstatd, to the Rebhan farm and introduce her to Martin's parents, then on to Aisch and the convent and see Sister Agnella," Betty added the final touch: "She and Gunda have been working on an agreement to have Sylvia stay with the nuns as long as it takes for us to straighten out our requests for a permanent US resident visa. We are going to have to wait."

This was news to me; of course it was more than that. There had been, it seemed, a flurry of communication among the adults. My mother had already written to the Mother-house in Neumarkt, and had made an offer to send funds there to cover my costs. My Aunt, Sister Agnella knew that Betty and Walter would be going back to the Rhineland where he could find work and establish residency. While there, they would be accommodating the time they would need for more than a visa. My mother assumed there would have to be the added weeks the Eigen's would need to make room and plans for an expected baby near Christmas. There would also be a need for some recovery time. The decision had been made among the adults; I could wait as well.

I can still picture the trek to the farm. There was a considerable amount of walking after another train ride. We crossed a huge field in the early morning before the heat became a factor. A river crossing was managed on a ferry with a hand-held tow rope—it seemed that we were going to the ends of the earth.

✡ ✡ ✡

"So this is Sylvia?" It was not really a question. My father's parents had little to say to Aunt Betty and even less to me. I sat in a chair and tried to sleep sitting

up again. I am sure there had to have been a meal.
I remember that beer was served from a huge pail; I
was too young of course, and wasn't allowed to taste it.
There are vague images of farm houses and smells.
My aunt appeared to be over-whelmed and within
two hours or so we were turned around and hauling
ourselves back across the river.

"You must come back," someone had said.

I wasn't so sure I would.

"Agnella is expecting us," Aunt Betty had offered
yet another excuse for leaving a place soon after we
had arrived. She dropped in a phrase that caught
my attention.

"It's better this way. Sylvia will have a longer
visit with her aunt and living there will be a good,
educational experience for her." Betty was speaking
rapidly in German.

I tried to keep up translating what she said along
with what I thought it would mean to me. I recognized my aunt's tone, if not her words. I held my
questions to myself until we were back on the train
to Ebrach. I had another internal conversation about
Aunt Betty with my absent mother.

"What ever it is that is going to happen, if *she*
wants it, it might not be that good for me."

———

CHAPTER ELEVEN

The Niederbronner Schwestern and their Convent

"SHE'S DARLING!"

"Adorable."

"Such a sweet face."

"How old is she?"

"How long will she be staying with us?"

"What's your name?"

They had clustered around me, chirping and cluck-ing in sweet tones. Truly, the Schwestern (Sisters) seemed taken with the child in their midst. I looked up at my Aunt Agnella for my answers. They asked me more questions than I had heard in two months of traveling. Still, I remained quiet. I had already been told that Sister Agnella would answer for me.

My aunt said something like, "She'll be seven in September, Sisters. Her mother and other family members were able to petition and arrange it all by mail. She'll be with us indefinitely, as the convent is the best place for the child to stay until her guardians, my sister and her husband can be ready to take her back to America." It was the first time I heard I wouldn't be going home to my mother—for a *very* long time. But then she did something I thought nuns would never do. Stepping between me and the cluster of dark, long dresses, she gave me an adult's silent command. Her face said, "Don't you dare speak a word," while her body turned back to the women—and she *lied*. She said, *"Her name is, Betty."*

Her hand was on my shoulder. It was squeezing me with additional conviction. "Say hello to the good sisters, Betty."

There were quick little kisses on my cheeks; and gentle, warm hugs to add to my confusion. *Someone* was going to stay with these nuns, I just wasn't sure who.

Right there in the convent hall, when the nuns had scurried away so that Agnella could take me to my room, I found the difference between Aunt Betty and this Aunt. Sister Agnella was going to *explain* the situation, something Aunt Betty was never able to do in our lifetimes.

We started walking down the hall while she talked. My room was not much bigger than my mother's closet in the Bronx. At the far end, a crucifix hung below a tiny window. Next to a bed there was a table, large enough to hold a small lamp; opposite the bed, a two drawer bureau. The floors were polished wood. Agnella had to assist me up onto the high, very firm mattress.

"Do you have something to say?" she asked. Remember, you may say it to me if you promise you will always come to me first, that you will listen and then do your very best to accept my answers. Do you understand," she said gently.

"Why can't I be 'Sylvia'?" I asked. It was my first question and my first test with a fuller truth than I had ever been given. "Why do I have to be, 'Betty.'?"

Agnella had a choice of answers. She might have pointed to my birth certificate, which still carried the name other than the one my mother had chosen, but she didn't. She could have tried to explain that she thought it was more pious since "Betty" was short for Barbara in German—and closer to being named after a saint. But she *didn't*. She told me the truth—Germany's truth.

"Our Mother Superior told me to give you another name when we first considered having you stay here." The story was not easy to follow, but I clearly remember the reason and the outcome. It was my first introduction to new German philosophy and the politics of the moment.

The Mother Superior in the Aisch Convent hadn't actually questioned the decision reached by the Mother house in Neumarkt; she knew better. But she had been quick to add her own directions. *Aunt* Agnella had categorized the tone; it was serious—and less than enthusiastic. The older nun had taken Agnella aside. "Keeping the child with us is more than a bit unusual, Sister," she had raised her hand, palm out for emphasis. "We are not a boarding home, nor would we consider keeping her with us except for the considerable contributions given to our Order—and the *circumstances*."

My Aunt Agnella had understood perfectly well, but she feigned ignorance. What was actually said between her, and her superior included the idea that the sisters had been generous to agree to let me live with them. My mother had been especially generous, too. Both she and her sister thought my staying there was infinitely better than being uprooted by continuous travel while Betty and Walter tried to renew *that* visa. Because the convent held only Kindergarten classes, the local school would provide a first grade education, and the nuns could see to my spiritual needs.

On the surface, it looked good. But it was the beginning of my *"disappearance."* Agnella told me she had offered a mild enough thought. "I think you'll find the child is very well behaved. She's sweet, very attentive—and very quiet. She won't be any trouble, you'll see."

In return, the convent administrator and spiritual leader warned, "Well, see that she isn't." The Mother Superior had flexed her fingers and pointed

in Agnella's direction. "You will have to take charge
of her. I have already noticed that we must do something about her table manners. I suggest she sit in
the kitchen until she can handle a knife and fork."

Agnella had spoken to me in soft tones for most of
this story, but she started to whisper the rest. "We had
to change your name because the Mother Superior...
well, she thought it wasn't a good idea to have you
use it. She thought that under the *circumstances*..."

I didn't understand the word.

Agnella seemed very uncomfortable, she stumbled
as she went on to say, "Our countrymen have concluded that we must avoid...stay away from...there are
people who we cannot...we have to be willing to choose
people that are truly—German—above all else."

She seemed to know what I would ask next. "Now,
both your parents were born here, good Christian people, but your name...the Mother Superior doesn't want
anyone to get the *wrong* idea. Your name, 'Sylvia,'
well, she thinks it sounds—too Jewish."

———

CHAPTER TWELVE

The Littlest Nun

UNCLE WALTER'S REALITY was being adjusted in a different way. His trips to several embassies resulted in rejection of his wife's appeal. Hers—and in fact, his country of birth had other matters to deal with. Today I know that a series of events, years of angst and acumen had led to a diplomatic failure. It was reported in all the newspapers that certain *wrongs* would be *righted*; the German military might had been unleashed. Among borders at issue were those of Czechoslovakia. Before the summer was over, its land and its people had been "annexed." By September Walter was reading about Poland. Unwilling to be swallowed whole, the Poles were forming an attitude of resistance. There followed a savage and consuming attack by German forces. This "Blitzkrieg," as it came to be called, the swift attack by air and ground troops set the world powers in motion.

In personal terms, it stymied us as travelers. Told that the matter would be settled in a matter of weeks,

Walter and Betty reconsidered the decision to leave me at the convent. They drew the same conclusions. I was supposed to be better off there until these "political" matters could be settled. The rejection by the nun's of my culturally-inconvenient name was obscured by my family's need to "get along." Truly, I don't think Aunt Betty was aware of the darker implications, and if Walter was, he never acknowledged them to me. Their acceptance of a behavior to fit German circumstances was more simply put. "Well, whatever it takes—it won't be long now."

I know that as a seven year old, I didn't have the depth to accept or reject what I was told. My disappointment was in giving up my name. While I am fairly certain my Aunt Agnella was not political, I do think she had spiritual reasons for being embarrassed by the convent policies, certainly where I was concerned. It wouldn't be the last time we would talk about German certainties. I say 'talk about' because I wasn't old enough or smart enough to grasp the full meaning of her dismay. I liked her. I wanted to stay with her. Yes, the name, 'Betty' would have been my *last* choice, but as long as it was hers, I would try to be the "little, well-behaved child" she had said I was. I know I wanted to stay at the convent—I really did. It was not like anything I had known; it was a world unto itself—and I believed, at least, that Aunt Agnella wanted me there.

✡ ✡ ✡

My meager belongings were moved to my room off a long hall, my wardrobe returned to me in spurts, after most of the short *American* skirts were lengthened with crocheted borders to cover my knees. Someone had rejected them as "immodest." There were other considerations more to my liking. Agnella, having known that the doll carriage would stay at Papa Ruppenstein's in Ebrach, conspired to find a replacement. For my seventh birthday celebration with the convent's Kindergarten children, my presents included a sweet, new, smaller baby buggy made of wicker. Betty and Walter remained nearby and joined in the celebration. Confident that I would settle in, they at least waited to see me safely into this new environment before leaving.

I went by myself on the first day of school and all the days after. The dirt path from the convent through the village of Aisch led directly to a school house. Before going west to the Rhineland, Aunt Betty came out to the convent to have her picture taken with me. I was dressed up, wearing a matching hat and coat, my Sunday paten-leather shoes and high white socks. I had a limited wardrobe, but I wore my best. Actually, *all* that I had was "my best." Someone had provided my school bag. I carried the stiff, cardboard back pack covered in brown leather that held my slate, several pieces of white chalk, and the "eraser" I had knitted with a crocheted edging. It was attached to the slate tablet by a long piece of wool. The nuns had added a lunch.

The pathway to the school house was direct and led through the village beyond the convent, and I was not afraid of getting lost. I *was* afraid of the nasty group of geese that patrolled the small village street, hissing and running along beside me. Born a city girl, I tried everything, clapping, whistling and shouting; the geese were resolute. The thought of missing the beginning of the school day gave me courage to risk going on. I started to run, darting left and right and not stopping to give them any advantage. Short of breath, I finally made it through that gauntlet and burst through the school's front gate, a makeshift sort of planking that at least served as a barrier between me and my pursuers.

Several of the school-aged children were there ahead of me. I was overdressed; they were wearing ragged shirts and shifts. They were gathered outside the school room in a small five-by-ten-foot area flanked by long wooden benches. Most of the children were seated having divided themselves in unequal groups, some to the right and others to the left. Huffing and puffing from my race to remain un-pecked by the geese, I tried to choose which side to line up on, what to do, when the biggest girl rose from her seat and asked, "Who are you?" Outside the convent wall, and completely unsure of myself, before I could choose between "Sylvia" or "Betty," the monitor rushed on. "We're going into religious training before our classes." Pointing to the line-ups on the benches along the wall, she demanded to know on which side I belonged. "Are you a Protestant or a Catholic?"

Unaware of my motivation; even as I was more than aware that the nuns and Aunt Agnella were Roman Catholic to the core, I also knew they wouldn't let me be *who* I was. My answer reflected a deeper identity than anyone could have imagined.

I surprised myself. Raising my head, I looked her straight in the eye and replied—in English—"I am an American!"

———

CHAPTER THIRTEEN

Where Is Sylvia?

SISTER AGNELLA PROVED to be the "smart" sister. She knew everything. She knew answers to questions I never thought to ask. Other nuns stopped her in the long halls, their voices low, practically soundless. When several huddled around her, their voices blended into requests that approached humming. She was the conductor of activities, her long fingers pointing in emphasis, she appeared to direct the chorus.

"Quiet as a mouse," she urged me, moving her finger from in front of her lips down and around to the back of her skirt. I would fall in behind her, careful to stop when my aunt did, hidden from those we approached. I soon became persuaded that I *couldn't* be seen. When Agnella wanted me, she would appear in a doorway, crook her finger, and "Betty" would join her in what I came to believe was our next escapade. We went everywhere, together.

One Sunday morning after the birthday party, Agnella signaled from the kitchen doorway. I knew to leave the rest of my breakfast and go. I dabbed at my mouth with a big cloth napkin as I rose, but Agnella fluttered her fingers at a nearby nun who scooped me up to rinse my fingers and almost drown me with equal handfuls of water on my face. It was unusual. I remember that I was not bathed often. Sponged clean, I was spurred forward, packed into a sweater and pushed through the door to my aunt's outstretched arms. They were full.

"You will carry my music," Agnella explained. "I don't need to tell you how important it is that you don't drop a single sheet."

The pile of books and papers was two inches thick. I held on to it as if it were one of her babies.

The early morning air still clung to the wet tips of grass in a movable mist that parted before my straight-backed leader. Alone, and out of ear shot of the convent, Agnella turned. "Sylvia," she said with an impish twist to her head, "just march along with me. Out here, you are my dear niece." I was so thrilled, I never asked where we were going; rather I just followed a narrow dirt road through a stand of trees and along a series of furrowed fields. We had been on foot for half an hour before we came to a small cluster of buildings, one of which drew special attention. I swallowed the strong odor of many loaves of bread cooking in an oven; the few people who appeared to be in the narrow street were coming and going to a bakery. My nose remembered; home and Mutti. Further along there were other structures, small houses and a building with a general store front. We hadn't passed by more than ten buildings when we came to a large, two-story structure built of stone.

"This church is in the village of Adelsdorf," Agnella offered, "I come through here every week," she added motioning for me to follow as she mounted a long stone staircase attached to the outer wall. She urged me upward. I worked hard to maintain the pace, but my legs were so short that my knees banged into the bundle of music as I climbed sucking in the damp air. The staircase had no railing, but the height wasn't of any concern. I didn't want to be left behind.

Sister Agnella led me through a wooden doorway and across a planked floor to a piece of furniture at the edge of low wall. It was a large wooden arch encasing layers of white and black keys. I thought I was looking at a pile of pianos.

"Haven't you ever seen a large organ before?" Agnella whispered.

I shook my head.

"Well this is one," she pointed, "and I play the keys with my hands and all those pedals with my feet. I play for the people who come to Mass here on Sunday. Look behind you; those are the organ pipes that make the sounds, the music you will hear when I play. I warn you. It can get pretty loud up here."

We were standing in front of a line of long, golden pipes some of which reached to the highest part of the ceiling. I turned and turned again, looking at the walls, the windows patched with colored glass, the altar below, the great, huge crucifix. Agnella took the pile I had carried and placed it on a rack at the top of the organ and lifted me into a chair next to her own seat, a high wooden bench.

"You can get down and look if you promise to keep still, very still," she whispered. "We are in the church in the presence of our Savior." The sound of her playing filled the air and drove itself into my ears. It took less than a minute for me to recognize that I was in the presence of the musician in the family.

It was *our* routine. Sunday after Sunday right through Christmas, I found myself peering over the top of the short balcony wall. I could look down on the congregation filling the pews below, a batter of men, women and children stirring and swirling beneath me. I didn't have to be told to be quiet. I had surrendered my voice along with my name. I would have to *make do.*

From my perch high above the congregation, looking down, I had already made my choice. If I couldn't be with my mother, I was at least in some part of my own idea of Heaven.

✧ ✧ ✧

I had a dozen mothers, all at the ready to get me up in the morning, clothe, feed, and entertain me during the day, read and tuck me into bed at night. I reveled in the attention. Every day was exciting. At first,

I was only mildly interested, but I became obsessed with the nuns' smooth faces and soft hands—they were the parts of their bodies that weren't covered with dark, stiff cloth or the pristine white, starched head bands and bibs. I wanted to know what they looked like under those cowls and habits.

✲ ✲ ✲

Whether I slept on my side or back depended on how I had been tucked in. The nuns appeared to be trained to draw the blankets firmly over my body; so tight that in spite of their leaving my arms and shoulders out, I could barely turn. I managed to feign sleep one night, wriggled from my cocoon, went down the long hall that connected my tiny bedroom to the others, dropped to my tummy behind a corner and peered into a room where several of the younger nuns were getting ready for bed.

They all had hair, luxurious and long. I don't know what I thought of them before that night, perhaps that their clothing had hidden some sort of ugliness that they had to cover up to prevent anyone from seeing. I was shocked to see how beautiful they looked. In the dim light, without all their layers of black, they were full-figured, but slim. I thought I was looking at a painting. Only the idea of discovery made me break away and scoot back to my bed.

✲ ✲ ✲

I began to count my days in the kitchen. I wanted to eat at the "big" table; to do that, I had to master my cutlery. Certainly my fork work improved as soon as I heeded the command to hold it upside down in my left hand, put smaller portions on the back side of the utensil, and then raise the pile of food to my mouth, which I elevated to the proper height above my plate. The knife was not as friendly. When the sister who had been appointed as the chief-meat-carver pronounced me ready, I had been seven weeks-in-waiting. The fall season was practically over before I left the added heat of steaming pots of potatoes and the sizzling egg pans to join the adults at the dining room table.

✵ ✵ ✵

Everything was of interest, even the winter winds, which often drove the nuns indoors with their hastily collected laundry. One such day, I came upon a bevy of nuns pulling at long, rectangular cloths, stained pale pink, crocheted, spotted "flags" hanging on the line along with white shifts and pantaloons cracking in the wind. No one seemed prepared to tell me about this apparently monthly phenomenon.

I learned some of the other facts of life when I overheard older school girls discussing their bodies. Every once in a while, my inner instincts rejected some of what they had to say. I wasn't sure that I would come to believe as they had, many of them having already joined youth groups of girls who were hoping to menstruate, become women and have a baby for the "good of the country." At seven, I was too young to do more than be slightly interested. I remember thinking I wouldn't be in Germany long enough for it to be something I would have to consider.

Christmas of 1939 was supposed to be the Convent's finest moment. For weeks, the nuns had been preparing for a festive period with music and lights. The walls were decorated with greenery brought in from the out-of-doors. Holly and berries were everywhere. A huge tree had been set up in the largest hall and strung with candles, berries and paper ornaments. I was included in a series of masses in the chapel where busy and joyful nuns practiced music to celebrate the coming of the baby in the manger. While there would be celebrations in the Adelsdorf church, there was a huge procession into the small church right there in Aisch for a Mass at Midnight. Surrounded by grown ups preparing for a spiritual event, my expectations had never been higher.

I have to admit that I was disappointed the next day. A few months with the good sisters had not prepared me to be spiritually thrilled with my modest collection of Christmas gifts. I unwrapped a napkin to see the sum total of my presents—one orange, a chocolate bar and a cookie.

✡ ✡ ✡

January's inclement weather became a deterrent for any release in outdoor activity. Copious amounts of rain made the Sunday trip to Adelsdorf a hazard of spectacular proportions. Ground water poured down hills of the furrowed fields, flooding the narrow path on the way to the church. The phenomenon appeared to block the way, and there was considerable support for the idea of canceling the weekly trip as Sister Agnella and I approached the beginning of the expanse that had been covered by rushing water.

Men were calling out from the Adelsdorf side. They were making their way toward us by creating a bridge/walkway of planks snaking above the flood waters. It looked like they had used every available piece of wood, a rough hodge-podge that shook under their feet. I was told to go back, but watched on the convent side as Agnella went with them back across their makeshift causeway on stilts. I looked on in awe as she made her way across.

Agnella's methods were brave, innovative—and immodest. With strong men staggering before and after, she had pulled her habit skirt up between her legs and tucked it into the front of her waist band, creating billowing bloomers well above her knees.

At one point she climbed up on a strong man's back, her legs wrapped around his middle. As soon as the first hurdle of the trip was accomplished, the villagers watching on the far side respectfully turned to allow the nun to adjust her clothing, and then surrounded her on their way to the mass that had been slightly delayed. In the meantime, the water having increased in depth, presented an even more perilous return trip. Agnella remained resolute. I went out and down to the edge of the water. She repeated her performance as villagers applauded across the distance.

I thought she was magnificent.

————

CHAPTER FOURTEEN

If Winter Comes

I COULD ONLY imagine what was going on in America. I really didn't think about it that much or I've forgotten. It would take many more years before my mother had the opportunity to tell me.

"Where is your little girl? We never see her anymore. Where's Sylvia?"

My mother had grown weary, especially since her answer appeared to elicit more questions than she was prepared to consider. In spite of the unrest abroad, she still felt confident that I was safe with the good nuns; "considering the circumstances" meant something entirely different to her. No special attention was given to Agnella's decision to change my name—or the German menace posed to those who actually were attacked for theirs. What Mama had thought that *her* daughter was probably going to have to spend the entire school year away. Betty's letters carried news of the impending birth of a niece or nephew. When asked, my mother had no interest or knowledge of the "Polish business." She considered what the paper called it—the "Blitzkrieg," but thought it might end the quarrels among politicians and facilitate the return of her family.

At the moment, my mother was more concerned about my father.

Just after the New Year's Day, he had announced his intention to attend one of his "meetings," but had not come home for two nights in a row. Moreover, Mama and their helpers had to work in his place to set and bake the rolls and breads without him. She wasn't frantic. Their married life had settled into a routine. She thought his staying out was irresponsible, and she wasn't sure whether or not she wanted to hear from him, at all. He hadn't called, but the bank had.

Her day had gone badly.

"Look," she called out to the latest young man she'd sent for to fill in for her husband, "I have to go to the bank and then to the post office. I'll be back before three."

She didn't tell her temporary employee that the bank people had said there had been some "mistake" in the account. She was grateful for a lull in the winter's business as she would be gone longer than she cared to be. It wasn't a Friday, her regular day of deposit. Confident of her own, well-kept records, she was sure the business would be short in its duration, that the young people at the bank had made a clerical error—you had to watch these newcomers who often couldn't add or subtract—and she wanted to send along her monthly stipend for my care. She had already made out the envelopes, one to the mother house in Neumarkt and a newsy letter to me. She had addressed it to "Miss S. B. Rebhan" in a half-hearted attempt to placate Agnella who had asked her to. It was one of those issues that divided them. Mother's thinking was practical and immediate. She needed to know her daughter was in good hands, even if those hands were more religiously bent in a pious way than her own. She hadn't approached the seriousness of much of anything else.

Such a to-do over a name, she thought, her reference being the stiffness of her family. She thought her sisters, like her father had objected to her naming a child after the heroine in a love story she'd read, or they believed she had been influenced by the movie star Sylvia Sydney. She tried not to think of any other unpleasantness, hoping her good will would go along with her mail—and her money.

"I brought fresh rolls," she had offered with her characteristic smile.

"Oh, thanks so much," said the bank clerk. "I always appreciate what you bring me. How's little Sylvia doing?"

My mother had shared her baked goods and her better feelings with the clerk; they had known each other for years.

"I don't know how to put this," the bank teller had said with genuine concern, "I've checked and double checked for you, but..." she leaned over the high counter and lowered her voice. "You don't have sufficient funds to cover this check to the Hagopian Brothers, your butchers. Your account is overdrawn. I didn't want to tell you over the phone."

"Impossible!" Mother had been adamant. "Here, I just balanced this account with you last month. There are more than two thousand dollars remaining. Look for yourself." She pushed her bank book across the smooth marble surface.

"Yes, I remember going over those figures, but see," she pointed to the end of a column, "this balance doesn't reflect Mr. Rebhan's withdrawals this week."

"My husband hardly ever writes a check over twenty dollars. Even with his amounts left to be subtracted..."

"Mrs. Rebhan, your husband's checks totaled twenty-five hundred dollars. There is no balance. It's gone!"

"Gone?"

"Yes, and you will have to make a deposit to create a balance before you can write another check."

"But the flour bill, the vegetables..." she trailed off.

"I will personally hold any checks that come into the bank in the next few days, Gunda. You have been such a good customer, so reliable. We can give you a chance to cover any outstanding checks. Can you make a deposit today? Restore the balance?"

Even as she retold this story she would have to struggle to make her lungs draw in the frozen air that hung between her and the teller. She urged her mind to gather in all that she had seen and heard, adding it as she would a bill of sale.

Ka-ching, ka-ching!

She stepped back. "No," Gunda responded, not as my mother, but as a wife. "It's gone for good." With a clarity that her stoic Prussian father might have mustered, she reached for and closed the bank book, put it in her pocketbook, snapped the clasp shut, and added her final truth into the total.

"It's gone," she said aloud. "All gone...!" To herself she confided, "And so is Martin!"

Ka-ching!

☆ ☆ ☆

At home, Mama checked the bureau drawers, the bottom of the closet. My father hadn't taken all his clothes, just the better of his pants and shoes—and his brown shirts. She made a few phone calls; none of their more casual friends appeared to have any information, and she was loathe to say too much, concerned that what her husband might have done would truly reflect badly on her or the business. As discreetly as possible, she inquired about Bund meetings in New

83

Jersey, thinking he might have gone there. There remained one *real* possibility: Germany.

✵ ✵ ✵

Certainly, she didn't report him missing to the authorities. In a week's time, she had to admit that she thought she knew where he had gone. It was surmised that he had crossed the ocean. My father did not reveal the details with anyone prepared to share his secrets. It is supposed that, after the fall of Poland, he had approached his "friends," somebody who knew how he could quietly leave the country and get back to Germany. He had begun to plan.

If he had had any thoughts of buying a ticket and crossing the Atlantic on the Bremen, the ship was no longer available. Many potential passengers to Germany hadn't anticipated the budding friendship between the British Prime Minister, Winston Churchill and America's President Franklin Delano Roosevelt. Churchill had suggested that the two world leaders consider a way to prevent the blue ribbon ocean liner from sailing to Europe and joining the German fleet as a war ship. The possibility centered on Churchill's fear of a German invasion of the British Isles.

In August of 1939, the Bremen had sailed into New York. After the September action against Poland, the United States <u>un</u>officially intervened. The ship's October return to Europe was delayed until the arrival of a British cruiser meant to escort the ship back toward England, effectively removing her from the potential role as part of the German Navy. The captain informed the loyal crew, and it was reported they sang the patriotic, "Deutschland Uber Alles," as they sailed out of the harbor under the watchful eye of the British war ship. Instead of following the "plan," the 50,000-ton liner revved up its classic engines and sailed faster than the cruiser, managing to out-distance even the poised guns of the slower naval vessel. The escape was complete. Much of the crew left the liner in what was under a Russo-German accord, the neutral port of Murmansk. Safe in Russia, some of them spilled over the side with cans of paint. A camouflaged phantom slid along the coast of Norway arriving in Germany in December.

When my father "defected," he would have had to accept a furtive return. He had waited until after Christmas and then probably "hopped" a freighter, leaving my mother—already without her child, in debt, without immediate funds, and without a husband. As for Gunda-the-woman, there might have been a moment where she knew she could do better without him. She could only hope that she wouldn't regret letting me go to Germany. She would have to find a way to continue sending money to the convent, and Martin, well, she believed his time would come— he might end up in Hell.

———

CHAPTER FIFTEEN

On the Move to Somewhere

MY FATHER ENDED up in the German army.

My soul was being saved *for* me. Politics aside, the "good nuns" were preparing me for a First Holy Communion, a Grace still being made available for German children in the Roman Catholic Church. In spite of Rome's mixed response to the growing Nazi menace and what it presented to their interests, the newly elected Pope signed an agreement meant to protect the Vatican City and its priests and nuns. The Church still maintained its ceremonial tradition to offer the Body and Blood of Jesus Christ to baptized members whom they believed could distinguish right from wrong at the age of seven, me included. Moreover, the Bishop would be passing through the area later in the spring, and despite the "circumstances," it was decided to add on the Grace of Confirmation usually considered when a child was closer to twelve. I was taught to answer from memory since I could barely read all the German catechisms provided. I was anointed, "the devil slapped out of me" by the Bishop, and I was given my own small stein for beer at the dinner table.

I remembered liking the taste of the beer.

✡ ✡ ✡

Agnella took Walter's phone call. She had written about what must be done.

"We'll be there Saturday. Please have her ready."

Nobody said a word to little "Betty."

I guess none of them thought I needed to know where I would be going next. Certainly, no one said that my father took the family savings and had gone missing. Mama hadn't told them everything. Much, much later I learned that because of my father's appropriation of all the funds, the Mother-house checks stopped, and I was no longer a welcome guest.

I wasn't the first to leave that spring. I was told in a matter-of-fact manner that several of the nuns had left their religious surroundings for what they believed to be a greater good: to bear "superior" German children. These girls, barely more than children themselves had already been drawn into the major philosophy proposed by the Nazi regime that came to be known as a *Gleichschaltung,* where *every* facet of life would be controlled by the government.

When I asked where several of the younger nuns were, I was told they had left to have a baby for the Fatherland, for Hitler. I remembered my sex-education from the school girls; I thought a nun having a baby might have a good a reason to leave the convent. The details were lost on me. There were those girls, I learned, who could join a special youth camp where members of the elite military would sire their children without benefit of marriage. Many young women submitted their personal histories so they would be among the chosen. Most were blondes; they truly believed they were having babies for Hitler as part of a movement to produce a pure race. I didn't get it, especially the part where red heads need not apply. If someone had a baby with red hair, the family was horrified. It was a well-known but hidden fact. I knew it as it was told to me with the same conviction and zeal some nuns had used to teach me to say the rosary.

✲ ✲ ✲

"Where's Aunt Betty?" I had asked my uncle.

"She's with Sister Agnella, saying goodbye. We will be going back to the Rhineland."

"And then?"

"Child, what are you asking me?"

"And then, are we going to…go home?"

"Home?"

"To America, to Mama!"

"Not just yet, Liebchen. There are problems. Just some more time. You are going to stay with us, Aunt Betty and soon enough, your baby cousin. As soon as we have the permission..."

"We are not going home, are we?" I knew it!

His face was turned away. "I'll promise to tell you when we can go."

How could I tell him? On that day, I knew the best way to get by was to stop caring.

✵ ✵ ✵

The return trip to Ebrach presented the same travel problems as the beginning of our sojourn. Neither Aisch nor Adelsdorf had a train station. Walter flagged down a train going toward Bamberg. Another leg brought us to Ebrach. Like it or not, we would have to consider asking Grandfather to provide us with tickets west to the Rhineland. It wouldn't be that easy. His position as station master had taken on a new life of its own. He wasn't free to share the numbers of military travelers who would also be going west. Not privy to the politics of travel, I could only bear witness to the results of increased shortages at the dinner table. There, conversations centered on the acknowledged shortages of farm produce in the Industrial belt.

Walter and Betty had a plan.

Papa Ruppenstein was outraged. "Are you mad? My own daughter planning to smuggle and hoard? What happens if you get caught?" He had tried to appeal to Walter who had raised his hands in a mock surrender.

"Well..." the Prussian appeared equally helpless, "...then don't tell me a thing! I don't want to know about it!"

Chicken eggs, it seemed, were not being shipped west on "his" trains. He thought the shortages were temporary, and he wasn't prepared to listen to plans for his family members to carry a large supply back to the Rhineland with them.

I found the plan exciting! The "shipping crate" was to be my doll buggy. I watched with increasing interest as my aunt and uncle removed the carriage from my grandfather's cellar, dusted it off and pulled up the mattress and the board beneath it. They filled the huge cavity with a dirty gray substance that would softly cradle dozens of uncooked eggs. The gooey mass separating and supporting them had been created by a gelatin mix. The board and mattress were wedged back in place; on top. My doll babies were tucked in, their blanket drawn tight. Evidently, the unheated luggage car would keep the mass a flexible solid. Walter's attention to our 'luggage' intensified. I was the only one of us who slept on that trip. I can still bring back the exhilaration I felt at being the owner that supplied the "treasure trunk." I knew instinctively that it was not a sin, nor would I confess it when I next had the opportunity to sit with a priest. I can confess it was my first illegal act; it wouldn't be my last.

✤ ✤ ✤

Safety was the operative word. My family had been told by the American Embassy personnel in Cologne, that as a young American child, I was safe where I was. Every expectation, it seemed, when shared in front of me, was that Betty's visa was not going to be available in the *near* future even as they still believed it might be, *eventually*. After all, they reasoned, Germany was not at war with America.

Plans shifted to considerations of sending me alone. Mother had tried to book passage on an American cross-Atlantic airplane, the Yankee Clipper, with a Lisbon destination. It was not to be. Queries about a child traveling through France to perhaps fly out of Portugal were dismissed after the declaration of the French government in support of the Poles. The French were speaking of furthering the fighting. Even the English were discouraging travel through waters about to be churning with submarines. No, my mother, Aunt Betty and Uncle Walter had wanted to believe that in Germany everything was under control, and everyone should continue to maintain an even disposition. *Safety first*! "It will all be over soon."

✥ ✥ ✥

Europe was in turmoil, and in the Bronx, the growing conflict affected German- Americans as well. Mother and her customers and suppliers all discussed the reality: I, a child could not return on my own, and my caretakers were under increasing and intensifying stress. They couldn't book passage without the proper papers, Aunt Betty was still a German citizen and under pressure to consider me as though I were *her* child—and *her* problem. Mama *was* aware of the fact that England had declared war on Germany and it meant that I was at risk. She would try her best to extract me. Her efforts were never going to be good enough.

A glass jar sat on mother's bakery counter. It was labeled, "Sylvia" and held a growing fund of contributions from customers. It was put there by one of Mama's biggest supporters, her butchers, the Hagopian Brothers. They had already shown her "special" assistance by continuing to deliver meats without immediate expectations of payment. They were willing to wait. The line was growing.

Other forms of patience would have to be developed where my return was concerned. There was no question that, as an American citizen, I could be allowed re-entry without my guardians, but the question still remained: How? On both sides of the ocean, the prevailing thought was that hostilities would be a quick succession of the blitzkrieg effect, and that Germany would soon end the conflict and come to some resolution with England and France. Everyone and everything else would have to wait.

The politics in the still-neutral United States were such that some German- Americans were growing fearful of reprisal from German nationalists in their midst; others were laying low, not wanting their own lives or livelihoods to be in jeopardy from Americans who questioned the increasing hostilities. Newspapers flashed headlines supporting hawks and doves, pro or anti French, English, and Russian. Many wished to stay above the fray and did not discuss the "strictly European problems."

On a personal basis, some of my mother's friends were beginning to be anxious about me. Some wondered why I had been allowed to go into an area that was "dangerous." Certainly Mama didn't know much about world politics, but a case can be made for her detachment and her reluctance to fear the worst. It wasn't her style to doubt the natural flow of family life. Those who had conjectures were left to assume that she had no real concept of the scourge that was blanketing Europe. Much of the talk centered on the thought that it was just a question of time—and money—before I would be reunited with her. On that note, deeply in debt and reduced to making small payments to vendors, my mother accepted all and any contributions for my return, but left them untouched.

Mama had other marketing hopes. If, in fact, the Giants Baseball Team did well in the spring and summer, then another World Series could be played.

Baseball might draw the bigger volume of customers she'd had in the past. She hoped the increase would make up for the business debts and the lack of a decent balance in her bank account. My poor Mutti. Even that thought didn't bear fruit. In 1940, the Giants did not win the National League Championship. There would be no World Series event for them up the street in the Polo Grounds—for years.

———

CHAPTER SIXTEEN

Border Closings

WALTER TOLD US he had stood in front of the diplomat's desk, his hands behind his back. He admitted trying to control the tremor that had taken hold of his fingers. It was the third time he had been in the office, yet the official had scarcely given his papers a cursory inspection.

"Yes, yes, well these seem to be in order."

The shaking stopped.

"Unfortunately, I won't be able to forward these to my superiors. Your wife is a German National. If you still want to leave right now, you will have to go without her."

"Without her? Without THEM?" Horst had been born just before Christmas. Walter was surprised at the thinness of his own voice. Whatever the delay, he was prepared to argue. It was going to be hard enough to get his wife, his son, and me home without making bad political choices. He was out of options.

"Well, young man, you must come to grips with this; the government is preoccupied."

Walter struggled to keep from protesting. He knew enough to curry favor. Remembering the lines he had stood in just to get his driver's license, he reflected that all officials were impressed with their position, regardless of the country; but in Germany he detected a more ominous note. He said nothing further.

Later, he tried to be more optimistic with us.

"No, we won't be able to return to the United States, just yet. I think the government officially believes its loyal German citizens will not wish to travel abroad in any case."

Walter wasn't going to go anywhere without Betty and his son; Horst was going to have me as his "big sister" until the war with England and France came to an end. It was Walter's opinion—everyone he knew agreed—that Germany had a superior force. It was just a question of time before the entire mess was settled. He had been told, "Come back in six months."

✵ ✵ ✵

I was close to eight. A year and one half had gone by, but I was no closer to being reunited with my mother. Instead, I was about to continue my elementary schooling and become literate in German.

My buggy had served its purpose as a ready-made egg closet; it stopped being a plaything. It was stored away for a time in an allotted space in the basement. Each apartment tenant had an assigned area. It was there we put supplies, our wood and coal for the stove, winter needs, potatoes, and other vegetables—and the eggs. They were stored in a big pail along with the transferred gelatin.

At first, my job was to move the eggs and the mixture without breaking any. It was more fun to reach in to the glop and retrieve them. I was also the go-for of all basement items. My other chores involved the one day a week allotment of the laundry facilities. The community washing machine had a manual attachment for wringing excess rinse water out of the clothing. It involved careful placement of items in such a way that turning of the wringer with one hand wouldn't endanger the fingers of the other. I'm not sure what happened to my carriage in the long run, but I know there was no room for it in the tiny Tönisheide apartment upstairs.

Two family houses on the street were attached in rows that were interspersed with an occasional four-story apartment house. The exterior of our unit was more in keeping with the typical "American," brown-stone; the interior was different, though. The second floor apartment boasted a large kitchen, one bedroom and an inside bathroom with running water. While each of the other two rooms was remarkably small, the kitchen served as an early version of a family room. It held: a porcelain sink and draining board under two wooden cabinets for dishes and glassware; a cast iron, potbellied, wood/coal-fueled stove with a flat top that could heat a skillet or a pot of boiling potatoes, but not necessarily both at the same time; a long table with four chairs; a day- bed/couch; and remarkably, an upright piano, which considerably reduced the walking-around space. The bedroom housed a wooden wardrobe, a crib, and one full-sized bed.

We all slept in the same bed, I next to the window, Horst between me and Betty, and Walter next to the door. On the coldest nights, heated bricks wrapped in ragged towels served to warm our feet. There was no central heating and these arrangements, if not particularly comfortable, kept us all from freezing when the weather turned cold. It was a totally different experience.

Bathing was a once-a-week occurrence. I sat in the baby's water—and Aunt Betty's water. Hygiene was not a top priority. I may have had a toothbrush, but brushing was not required daily. Perhaps that is why I had to go to the dentist who drilled into my teeth without benefit of pain killers. I didn't need go to the doctor; strangely enough, I was never sick.

I quickly learned that the neighborhood children knew I was a foreigner. Uncle Walter's sister-in-law lived with her son in a four-story apartment house across the street. From my sidewalk, I saw Tanta Friedchin in her spot at a front window where she could observe all the comings and goings on the block. She had her son, Werner living with her; he was four years older than I, and went off to a local high school leaving his mother with nothing much to do but watch over the neighborhood. I always thought that she, having so much time on her hands, might have been the one who told the neighbors that *poor* Aunt Betty had me living with her—"such a burden," and worse, that I was an American. With nothing much to do one day, I went across the street and walked up the four flights to see where she lived with Werner. I counted myself lucky as he was home and it was he who became my tour guide.

Mostly I remember the stench—the entire building smelled! While there had been running water in the kitchen, every toilet, one for each floor, was encased in a long tower/tube at the edge of a corner of the building—a sort of multi-storied "outhouse," which served to collect waste that dropped down from each floor to below street level. As much as I needed to relieve myself, I waited until I had crossed the street, thankful that our tiny space housed an indoor toilet with pipes to the sewer. Werner, who had come to ignore his own sense of smell, said my nose was decidedly, "American."

☆ ☆ ☆

There was a certain comfort in the architecture, the familiar paved street; it could have been anywhere off the Grand Concourse. One morning, free of my chores, I started off to examine the length of the block. Around the corner was a trolley line. I lingered long enough to watch a trolley, its overhead connector sparking against the cable. I thought it plausible that I could find something to do and walked back to join a group of six or so children playing curbside.

"Schweinhund!" a boy called out as I approached, "Americana Schweinhund!"

He was calling me a pig-dog, and the others began to howl and grunt German words I never had heard before. I began to back away. I wasn't so afraid that I hadn't begun to prepare my defense, but when they all stood, I was the smallest of the bunch.

I looked down the street toward the safety of my house. I knew I was a pretty good runner. My biggest mistake was to turn my back on them to try to get away. I was running, really running, and could feel them catching up. Turning my head to look over my shoulder, I saw twisted, animal faces, like the geese, only with flapping arms, and blunt beaks snipping and barking—and then I *was* afraid! I went down, tripping on a raised slate in the sidewalk. The pack piled on my flailing arms and legs, some one of them ripping the shirt from my back. My ears thundered from the sound of rushing blood, and I thought my chest would burst. There was no sound made by the air rushing from my throat.

I didn't even know what I could say to call out. My teeth—I thought—I am going to lose all my teeth. My shoulders pinned against the ground, the only frantic movement I could make was to scratch impotently on the sidewalk. My pain exceeded my anger. My world was a hurtful gray. Stomach fluid was at the back of my throat.

Blitzkrieg, I thought. I am dead!

I never actually saw what happed next. Above me, a small boy appeared to fly, propelled by some new raging force. First one and then another, the gang was pulled from my back and thrown away, sharp elbows and knees slapping against the ground. The air that raced back into my lungs burned so hot I lost my sight, but I heard the cries of the wounded. And then I saw him. Werner!

I had managed to raise my head enough to see my cousin's larger-than-life shadow on the street. It was a huge, black cartoon, hands on hips with one foot on either side of my nearly lifeless body. With the pile gone, he made one of the boys take off his shirt, and I can still feel him lifting me up and swaddling my upper body with it while he raged at my tormentors. "Cowards," he bellowed. None of them moved. He raised his right fist and shook it in the air with a wild swing, "See this, you bags of dog manure! This is what you will get from me if you touch this girl again! This is my cousin, Sylvia, and if you are mean to her, you are mean to me!"

He looked at each boy with the most menace I had ever seen in his face. "She lives here, now. And I will know if you are out-of-line in any way, and I will come for you! Get it?"

But what he said after that was incredibly wise. "You will let her be, AND you will make her welcome to our block, and what's more, you will let her join with you to play and have FUN!"

There was one mild protest from a defeated gang member. "But Werner, she's an American."

His reply seemed very appropriate.

"Oh that," he said. "Well she can't help it. She was born that way."

———

CHAPTER SEVENTEEN

Escalation

THE BACK YARD behind Werner's apartment house had been hung with old table cloths and tarps that turned ditches into forts. Protected by Werner, even during in his school-demanded absences, I joined the children in a typical day's activity. We played, war! We took turns being Germans, English and French. The Germans always won.

My life became routine; my routine—my life.

Baby Horst was nothing like a replacement for my dolls. He was round-faced and plump and might have been fun to hold when he was very small, but he presented a series of chores that I wasn't prepared for but had to do on a regular basis. I changed the dirtiest of his diapers, was responsible for keeping him happy, but as I was not his food source, he often screamed louder when *I* held him. He was more work than I really wanted to do.

My childhood memories of sheer fun dropped in the folds of my mind; some never went deep and other existed at the sharper edges. While I am not sure how Uncle Walter supported all of us, I think he must have gone to work locally. We could see the chimneys of the huge factories just to the west. My uncle had skills that were in great demand. Then too, some income must have come from Aunt Betty who taught the piano to an occasional student. She had little of Aunt Agnella's talent, but she insisted on trying out her methods on me. I was a reluctant learner having no interest in it on my own. Most days, both Walter and I left an unhappy and very agitated Aunt Betty; at least that's how I remember her when I went off to the local school. I came home in the afternoon and she took up the overseeing of my homework and further studies. She became obsessed with my schooling and took away my dolls. I coped with having real-life chores with the toddler, Horst. I was entered in a local school for second grade but I knew that *my* childhood was done.

☆ ☆ ☆

Schooling was changing under the new German government regime, but it remained open to the continuation of the private institutions for middle school students—the "Gymnasiums." Each of these schools throughout the country had an entrance exam that was severe; the select few who passed could attend.

Others were dumped into the general population of the new public schools. Aunt Betty talked of nothing else. I knew that Werner did not go to a Gymnasium. He pursued his studies in the public school system. He would finish the eight years there becoming a student of pharmacy—and he grew interested in bigger girls. He never abandoned me, however, and when he was home he inquired about my comfort level with others on the block. I seldom got to play *at* war. Real life was folding in upon us all—and Betty was intense and focused on my studies. She hounded me through the multiplication tables and my spelling. She believed that no child of "hers" should have a *common* education.

She wasn't too interested in how I looked. She was pregnant again! She often stopped braiding my hair long enough to be sick before she returned to brush it with firm strokes pulling at my roots. I had a few school dresses but my shoes continued to be a problem. Much of my American clothing had been adjusted for my height, skirts lengthened by wool added from some dismantled outfit. The nuns had taught me to wet and stretch wool, knitting it once again into strips that would provide knee cover. Otherwise, some of my clothing, with minor alterations, still 'fit.' Evidently, my contribution to the on-going war effort, oh yes, Aunt Betty kept using the word to complain—"war." I was to accept anything handed down for my use. Shoes that still had any life in them, no matter their size were "transferred." I remember stuffing paper in the toes of a too-large pair and wearing them for months until my feet grew. Even when enough money was earned, there was very little choice and practically no production of civilian footwear.

No one actually told me that France had capitulated, nor would the neighborhood children have processed the information in the same way as the world powers. It might have been enough to say that Uncle Walter and Aunt Betty knew there were two entities to consider; "Occupied," and "Free France." Getting me through the "Free" section still held its possibilities. In Germany, the French defeat had been a foregone conclusion. As for me, I did hear that German soldiers had marched into Paris. The unique part of that invasion, which remained outside my knowledge, was that in June of 1940, my father's wish had been fulfilled. He had always wanted to go to Paris. He was there with German troops marching under the Arch de Triumph.

My ninth birthday had been celebrated in advance of baby Ingeborg's, birth; now there were two babies to look after. My baby sitting chores doubled. Near Christmas, I sent a letter and card in English; it actually reached my mother at her new address. I had learned it by heart: 1109 Clay Avenue, Bronx, New York. Uncle Walter helped me write it. On the back of my letter, he told my mother that he had heard from my father, confirming that "Martin is in Germany and has joined the army." That is how I learned he no longer was with my mother, but thanks to my mother's hesitancy to share his outright thievery, his reputation was still intact. My father then became part of Aunt Betty's excited announcement, "Your papa is coming for a visit."

Aunt Betty knew nothing of mother's situation, just that that her brother-in-law was on leave, had taken a chance on reaching Walter's family in the Rhineland—and that we were there. I didn't know how to react. I hadn't had any contact with him for more than two years. It had been so long since anyone talked about him, I thought he must be dead. I had wished it was my Mutti who was coming to visit, that she would be taking me home. As for my father, well, I allowed myself a wide range of imaginative moments. I wondered if he was my Papa that *he* was coming for me to take me home. To tell the truth, mostly, I concentrated my thinking on the kinds of foods he would be bringing us. I could see the tins of sweets, French pastries, and canned meats. At last, I thought, enough food for all of us, as my being part of the Eigen family had made it more than difficult for my aunt and uncle's pantry. The government had instituted rationing as a universal "good" for the country. As a "legal alien" I could go to school; I had

German born parents; but as a non-citizen, without a German birth certificate, I was not entitled to food ration stamps.

My father arrived wearing a soldier's uniform. I *was* prepared to be glad to see him even though I scarcely could identify him. I don't remember anyone saying anything about my mother. Certainly, *I* was not the center of attention, either. There were no trinkets or special treats for his "little girl." Worse, he had been busy being a soldier—and he would be leaving without me. Even as I digested those facts, I held out for the grand opening of the two suitcases he was carrying. One contained his clothes—and oh, I had such high hopes for the other, which I was sure would be a treasure trove of my Parisian treats—until he opened it. It was filled with bottles of French wine that he had "appropriated" for his visit.

I may have been the one person at the table who *was* disappointed.

✡ ✡ ✡

For the most part, I settled in to a school routine that included a new found acceptance of my "situation." My father was not going to take me back to the United States, or to live with me in Germany. Nor were there any appropriate means of getting me across the ocean, never mind actually reaching the coast. I had no way of knowing that my second—and third grades would be the longest uninterrupted period of my fragmented schooling—and that they would take place in Germany.

The rest of that first year in the Rhineland is hazy. While I have fleeting memories of walking to school, carrying my lunch, playing at recess, making friendships and learning, I think I absorbed that year by swallowing it whole. I am pretty sure that there was some correspondence with my mother, but letters took forever and I may have given up on her—as much as I had given up on any of the adults in my life.

My school teachers were Germanic disciplinarians of the highest order. Still, they were no match for Aunt Betty's unyielding hounding, even as they accepted nothing less than perfection in the classroom. Like other students, I took pleasure in lunchtime and recess, making friends with classmates and running around until the big bell over the door rang and sent us back to add and subtract with what I noticed was a Germanic vengeance.

The skies over the Rhineland had grown smoky. Near-by factory production lines were running night and day to produce the hardware to support the Government's growing desire to increase its sphere of influence. Uncle Walter came home later and later and had less and less time to consider any plans to change his immediate situation. One day led to another, and life took another of its turns. Because he and Betty had two babies of their own, certainly the immediate future was "out of his hands." Like his neighbors, he had begun to believe that the noise in the sky made by the increase of German aircraft to the air above him would shorten the duration of what was still a "European" conflict. Then, the government added another factor; it "closed" the borders. Aunt Betty, the babies and others like her with German citizenship were going to have to stay put, regardless of their former plans.

The 1941 summer recess brought few change in my routine. It wasn't that warm, but there were a few opportunities where it was necessary to cool off in a bathing suit. By then my body had changed enough from my eighth to ninth year and my suit didn't fit. The problem was solved by cutting it in half and adding a bright red band of material in the middle. I wrote to my mother about my capacity for tailoring. It may have been the last letter she received. After that, she would have to go three and one-half years wondering what happened to me.

My mother had developed a new mindset. All her efforts to get me home had failed miserably. More and more of the family's letters from abroad centered on the reasonableness of my staying put. She believed that it was like sending her daughter off to boarding school, and it all would work itself out when Germany settled its differences. She would have to accept the status quo. She left the jar on the counter—accepted the support of all who cared about her well being, and kept herself hard at work. It would take months of silence from abroad to alter her comfort level. Later, she would come to assume a new level of despair.

———

CHAPTER EIGHTEEN

The Enemy Within

BY SEPTEMBER OF 1941, my ninth birthday, I was learning to make other adjustments as well. Along with my regular chores, I was assigned a new set. Baby Horst and his sister, Ingeborg needed me—and Aunt Betty had a new round of "heart palpitations." She settled on making me into an educated wonder child. My limited relief would come in satisfying her with my acceptance to the German equivalent of Middle School—a Gymnasium.

✡ ✡ ✡

The mail service sank into the ocean along with British tonnage. Not one of the correspondents could count on a reply if a rare letter managed to cross the seas. While Mama had hoped for a Christmas greeting, she hadn't had any messages in months. She had an added set of complications to worry about.

Early on December sixth, her radio had shouted out more disturbing news. Japan had bombed the U.S. Naval Station in Hawaii. She was stunned by the announcer's description of ships being sunk in the Oahu harbor; she winced with every phrase, casualty report, and "burning oil," "sailors trapped"—but her sense of horror drove her down onto the carpet when President Roosevelt asked the Congress to make a declaration. Japan was part of the German Axis. America was going to war! Those who had cautioned restraint in Europe no longer had a voice. But my mother *knew* the way of it. As an American citizen, I would be affected. Overnight her child had become an *"enemy* alien."

So it seems had Uncle Walter. He knew what the attack on Pearl Harbor would mean to *his* family. He made a tortured decision to save us politically and economically. I came home from school to see him handing new German rationing cards to Betty. With two citizenships, he had chosen to take his birth certificate to the local office of distributions. He had registered as a German. He hoped his action would make him a provider—and not a candidate for prison or a detention center.

At the same time, I would have to disappear into another level of "impersonal" or "non-personal" existence. Without a German certificate, I was not the recipient of any government assistance. My uncle and aunt would have to average me into all their quotas. There appeared to be one benefit. As an alien *child,* I would not be sent off to a camp for enemies of the state. And, I was also "unfit" to join the growing organizations of Hitler Youth. I was <u>un</u>official. Actually, I was relieved. My status left me free to play with neighborhood children and continue to go to school without going to all those meetings afterwards. But, there was the resurgence of Aunt Betty's afternoon activities to make me a young genius.

After the summer of 1942, I was tested and accepted by a Gymnasium in Velbert. On days when Aunt Betty had the fare, I took the trolley; otherwise I walked the nearly two miles there and back. In school, I was taught math, history, geography, and strangely enough, English. Whatever the challenge, I remember being grateful when I didn't get home in time to practice the piano!

✠ ✠ ✠

The early morning of the first Allied bombing on German soil far to the north and east was a mild intrusion. A series of rumbling rapports might easily have been connected to a growing storm in the distance. Still, the bass drum-like insistence woke Horst. In our bed, the motion of one roused another.

"What was that?" Horst wanted to know.

"Hush," I cautioned, "It's nothing." I was half right. It was nothing—compared to what it would grow to be. Night after night our sleeping became fitful anticipation of the next day's activity. The orchestration grew to include more than planes passing overhead; we were introduced to the sounds of bombs hitting their distant targets and antiaircraft guns shaking the earth. Soon enough, the nearby industrial complex was added to closer targets in the Rhine Valley. It was just a matter of time before local sirens whined us all to attention. The nearby landing of bombs, the whistles, the cracking apart of cement reached into the town and the citizens became equals in terror! We began to take cover in the cellars beneath the houses.

Compared to the children's, my aunt's reactions were heightened. She made no pretenses to cover her fear of "death from the skies." As the number of bombs and bombings grew, she became increasingly agitated. Alone, with my uncle often having to take shelter on his way back from the factory in which he worked, she began to shed layer after layer of decorum and appeared to be an exposed set of raw nerves. When the sirens sounded the all-clear, she was unable to go out. She sent *me* to get food and water from a government truck when the water supply lines were damaged. In more than one area, electricity was interrupted, and the quality of life reduced. In our neighborhood, the threat of bombs outweighed the precise landing of them. I wasn't the only child released to do the running for foodstuffs, but the possibilities of harm were heightened by the pounding taken at a distance.

✿ ✿ ✿

I learned that "war" was noisy, and would get noisier. At first, the British were bombing the factories by day, and the Americans chased us into the cellars at night. Then the bombings became constant. The sirens howled and howled. There, we were all potential victims of explosions that couldn't distinguish the worthiness of birth. The basements of buildings with a common wall were connected by newly made "doors" to an adjacent cellar. Bricks had been removed to allow passage from one cellar to another in the row, giving residents a series of alternatives. If a nearby building was hit, we could scurry through to another. Each unit was turned into some sort of living space. When sirens went off, the family would scramble out of our bed, we only had the one, and race below dragging covers of some sort. Ultimately, a variety of belongings simply stayed below street level.

At first, my reactions were not like those of local people. Instead, I was reminded of Candlewood Lake in the United States and our summers swimming and picnicking; the evening fireworks. Every night sky in the Rhineland was the like the Fourth of July. Searchlight beams stretched up into the blackness. Shells that exploded high above me released puffs of black smoke and shards of light. I was excited, but then, what did I know? Aunt Betty tried to control her screaming and carrying-on, but it was no use. I tried to calm her, my logic being based on a simple fact of my existence. I would take shelter with her in the day—who knew what the British might hit with *their* bombs? But at night, with Walter in the house, I was an *American,* and I believed with all my heart that "my side" wasn't going to kill us.

My resolve remained unshaken until one day the local children announced a discovery. Around the block behind Werner's apartment building, we had a real-life toy to play with. The long fuselage of an airplane that had crashed into an apartment house was creating a crowd of onlookers and fire brigades. The children stood memorized for hours standing-by for a chance to examine the remains of the larger-than-life aviation wonder. The next morning, I joined the neighborhood explorers scrambling up the cooled rubble as we picked our way through this spoils of war. We might just as well have been playing pirates in a far away azure sea. There were dials that, while blackened, still held readable numbers; scorched steel revealed written labels. My interest was peaked, my imagination challenged—and then I saw it—a tiny but recognizable image. It was an American flag!

✵ ✵ ✵

Betty was increasingly agitated. She began screaming at everything and everybody. She surrendered to her cultural leanings protecting mothers and her own fear. She sent me out without thought of the measure of destruction. Around the corner, sometimes the broken mains filled the street with water. Other days, the damage was minimal. Our block remained intact. At a distance however, Betty never considered that ultimately I might have to make my way past the remnants of human life.

I saw more than the occasional battered buildings. The wreckage was going to grow to include bodies. I knew that I would have to ignore loss of life. As long as I didn't know anything personal about them, I could release the dead in the street to God, and if necessary dart around them.

Having waited as long as she could, Betty convinced Walter to begin packing. She had her own convictions and definitions of the "enemy." We would all have to get away. Betty and her two babies were going to go with Walter, and I was going to go with them. We would try to get on a series of trains, and head east to Bavaria, Agnella and safety.

There was no contact with the outside world. What we knew of the progress of the war was what circulated with those of us ducking into cellars. Nobody had to tell me what I already knew. If the heavy bombing moved our way, pretty soon there wouldn't be anything—or anyone—left standing. It was the beginning of a very different mind set. *My* Americans weren't going to kill me; but sooner or later those bombs might.

———

CHAPTER NINETEEN

Narrow Escapes

"WHO'S 'SYLVIA'?"

He had come into the bakery every morning for a month once school was out, and never spoken more than the few words he needed to order one sweet roll. Mama made the connection; she'd actually had the roll put aside. Surprised by the form of his question, she hesitated before putting it in a bag. The boy's eyes barely met the height of the counter, but they were fixed on the jar. Like many of her customers he was a dark skinned Negro.

"How old are you?"

"I'm eleven."

"Sylvia is your age; she's my daughter."

"So where's she at?"

"She's in the middle of the big war across the ocean. We don't know exactly where, though."

"So why you got money in that jar with her name on it?"

"My friends, the people who come in here are try-ing to help me find her—and bring her back home." She couldn't help it. She thought she had steeled herself against any extra flow of emotions. Still, in front of this child, she began to cry. Pulling her eyes away from his, she looked at the money he had put on the counter.

"You gave me a nickel. The roll is three cents."

He took the two pennies change and the bag she had pushed in his direction. He turned to go, looked in his hand and returned to put the two coins back on the counter's glass top.

"You should put them two cents in that jar."

Running her fingers over the surface of the coins, my tough-minded, business- woman mother found her hands trembling. "You are a very generous young man to share these with Sylvia and me. Do you share that sweet roll with anyone?"

"Yes'm. I give some to my sisters."

"How many in all?"

"They's five of us—and Mom. She takes a pinch with her coffee."

"Well maybe you should take this change home to her."

"No, I think she would want to get Sylvia out of that war place. You can put them pennies in that jar."

"If that's what you really want." She lifted the coins, putting one in each hand, and dropped them gently. "Wait," she called him back. "What's your name?

"Joseph, but they calls me, Joey."

"You forgot your prize, Joey."

"Prize?"

"The Good People prize," she said cramming a big bag full of assorted rolls from the counter display. She held them out.

"I dunno if I should. What'll I tell my Mom 'bout all them rolls. She may say I took 'em."

"You tell her they're from my Sylvia and me." Mama said, pulling back the bag long enough to write, "Good People" on it with the big flat pencil she kept next to the register.

"Thanks," Joey said, offering a broad smile to everyone in the group of people that had been in line behind him.

"You're welcome."

And he was gone.

A large woman from the nearby apartment was next. "Gunda, you may be sorry you gave all those rolls to that Negro boy for two cents. He'll come back expecting them, regular like."

"And he'll get them!" my Mutti had responded.

"So, are you going to give me a dozen for two cents?" She winked.

"Don't be silly," the Gunda-person said, wiping her eyes with a corner of her apron. "Don't be silly."

✿ ✿ ✿

The Bavarian nights were quieter, filled with country sounds, animals at a distance, stars and clean, cool air. As before, we traveled first to Bamberg on a series of trains and then back-tracked north where one set of tracks led past the clearing outside Adelsdorf. What I could carry, what Horst could drag behind him and what Walter and Betty toted along with Ingeborg was the sum total of our transferable belongings. We left the Rhineland apartment knowing that it might soon be occupied by another homeless family with no way to leave the area. We had eaten little, and slept even less in order to get from one train to another on our ragged path east.

We walked the dirt road into Aisch, hoping that Agnella would assist us in finding adequate housing. Evidently, Grandfather Ruppenstein's was out of the question. It was Betty's decision not to ask her father to share his house with her family. There hadn't been anything available in Aisch, but her sister used her goodwill with people in the area to find the family a place in Adelsdorf; it hadn't changed. The townspeople still gathered for Sunday Mass. As for reminding anyone that I was the American child, "Betty," it was agreed that the less said about *her* origins and status, the better.

✡ ✡ ✡

The family quarters on the second floor were as sparse as our luggage. Horst, now nearly three, and his baby sister, Ingeborg nearing two, Betty, Walter and I would again have to share one bed—and a much smaller stove—in one room. Ironically, we were over the section of the building that housed the bakery. Our sense of well-being and our reaction to the aromas drifting upward depended on whether or not we were going to share in the daily bread ration. Mrs. Been, our landlady was an avowed church goer, and a devotee of organ music. Mr. Been, the baker, like many other villagers, had gone to the war to fight for the Wehrmacht.

Walter's family and I also shared the Been's "bathrooms." One was an outhouse, the other, a far cry from the Rhineland apartment's running water, but indoors nonetheless—a metal pot with a lid. Out of diapers, the children added to its contents. It quickly became my job to empty the pail in the morning. To get outside with our wastes, I had to descend the stairs and walk straight through the portion of downstairs allotted to the bakery in front of Mrs. Been's set of rooms, and go out the back door. Soon after my first day at this job, having tried a brief attempt at amenities, I learned to keep my morning greetings and apologies to myself. It's just the way it was.

There were other factors more pressing than hygiene. Walter, having already had a serious choice to make when under pressure to maintain the family in the Rhineland, had used his German citizenship and birth certificate to secure work. While he wasn't aware of it at the time, his choice had resulted in his automatic surrender of his American citizenship. Basically, in Germany, at the bottom of any recruitment commitment early on, he was swept up in a general civic order for able bodies, no matter their age or fatherly status. He was "drafted" into the German army.

✡ ✡ ✡

The status quo was under fire in America; *a* war broke out in Harlem—not an extension of the Allies vs. the Axis—no, a local conflict. Negroes in New York City were rebelling for a number of reasons not the least of which were *their* circumstances. Harlem, a section of real estate north of Manhattan, an area from 145th to 155th Streets, and often described as being bordered by Amsterdam and Edgecombe Avenues, had kept its Dutch appellation, Haarlem, with one less "a." Just as several sections of the greater metropolitan area had drawn similar ethnicities, Harlem had long been home to Negroes who had fled north before and after their emancipation following America's Civil war. Forty years removed from slavery had not begun to solve all the problems of racism, nor raised the economic level for many of the newer generations living far from Southern influences, even though those in service to their country were relegated to support jobs as military servants, corpsmen, cooks, and adjuncts. In the summer of 1943, their patriotism was not at issue. The end of this sort of segregation and the absorption of patriots of color into the regular ranks would extend long beyond the hostilities. The Bronx had been simmering for a long time from among other indignities, the conspicuous overcrowding of housing. School-age young people sought relief on the steaming Bronx streets and their brownstone stoops, a name given to outside stairways regardless of the number of steps.

Most historians agree that a July incident of questionable actions occurred as a result of interaction between a Negro soldier and a white policeman. Reports gave rise to a series of rumors that lit the fodder for an uncontrollable reaction in the Harlem community. Among those white citizens considered as neighborhood "enemies" were local merchants who were blamed for price gouging, black marketeering, and other conspicuous racial inequities. It was a violent part of a continuing battle for civil rights. Roving bands of Harlem youths were "making trouble," working their way toward the outer fringes of the area—and Mama's place of business, her bakery.

On her way to work, early in the morning, she had passed several gesturing boys who appeared to be without a plan, but evidencing potential for the destruction and retaliation that would follow. Mother called the police as soon as she opened the store. The phone line was busy. She would not get municipal assistance that day.

At the store, she made a practical decision. "I want you to take this money," she said pushing the cash register change into the baker's hand. Shaking the contents of Sylvia's jar into her apron, she hastily rearranged the few bills into a neat pile, which she counted and gave him. "Go downtown on the bus," she cautioned. Her back-room radio was keeping them updated, urging listeners to "stay away from the entire area." Fortunately, the Polo grounds' schedule had the Giants out of town for the day. The two men took turns begging her to leave with them.

"No, I'll be safe. You take the money...what are they going to do to a woman? I can't leave, I just can't." She wouldn't! When the men were gone, she stood at the window looking after them, hoping they would hurry away.

I heard one of several explanations of what followed: It was an hour before she saw a small group of boys making their way up the block. They were using bricks, and curbstones torn out of the sidewalk to smash plate glass windows in store fronts. She could see them crawling into the stores and taking items at will. The looting, slowed them down, even seemed to stop the forward flow. Relieved, she put her head down on a table, suddenly exhausted by the anxious looking and anticipating. A gentle knock on the pane pulled her head up. It was Joey. He had two huge black men flanking him like bookends. He was gesturing for her to open the door. For one sickening moment she felt she had been cheated, that he knew about some money in the register—and that jar, that he'd led the men right to her. Enraged, she pulled open the door, ready to fight for the money that wasn't even there.

"What do you want? There's been no baking here today."

"These are my uncles," Joey answered. "We figured we could stand guard."

"Stand guard?" The men were carrying what looked like mop handles.

"Yes," he said, "we're gonna stay all day and make sure no one bothers you."

"You don't want anything?" She was incredulous.

"No ma'am, unless you got a sweet roll or two left over from yesterday." He winked.

She found a few. Throughout the day, the trio stood at the ready, chasing a few youths by shaking fists and sticks in their faces. Once or twice she brought them water; fed them, even let them in one at a time to use the toilet. They stayed until well after dark.

No one really knows any longer whether or not "Joey" was the one of my mother's younger customers who actually kept the roving bands away. The story became one of a series of explanations for the good will between her and her neighbors. What is an *absolute truth* is that throughout the mayhem, her bakery remained one of the few undamaged businesses in her war in the Bronx.

———

CHAPTER TWENTY

News at Six

FOR MY AUNT, early on, there had at least been a few letters from Walter. His basic training had been the subject of some news, which she had shared with me in an attempt to spread Walter's comfort over the empty space in our lives. Then, like the overseas mail, service was suspended; the letters stopped altogether.

I don't know where it came from, but Betty managed to get her hands on a small radio. She was desperate for news of the eastern front and some word of Walter. She warned me that it was against the law to listen to any news broadcast by a station other than those approved in Berlin, but for the most part, the strongest radio bands traveled the airways after dark, courtesy of the British Broadcast Company (the BBC). From the German stations during the day, we were assured that the war was going to be won, by Germany—in the long run. I heard Hitler's voice many times assuring HIS people that Germany was working on a HUGE secret weapon, one that would turn the tide of the war.

From the British we heard a different story. Many German cities had been destroyed from the air. European land had been invaded by the Allies, the British and Americans having made their way through Africa and Italy. After years of Allied attacks on the civilian populace, an indignity they had been promised would never happen, German support for the war was ebbing. Locally, we were learning about the growing influence of the German secret police, the Gestapo.

Newly aware of the penalties and the power of the police, early in the morning, we wrapped the radio in a piece of oil cloth tied with string and put it inside the waste pail. I carried it down past the bakery area, followed by Betty and Horst who for all intents and purposes just looked as though they were making their way to the out house. I climbed down a ladder into the cesspool while Betty and Horst lowered the radio on a rope. I buried it deep under the surface of urine and feces. We followed the same procedure more than once.

✵ ✵ ✵

Food and the lack thereof became an increasing seasonal problem. We were in the heart of farmland that suffered from the weather and the lack of farmhands. Crops were hard to plant and more difficult to harvest. Local children became part of a contingent of genteel beggars. The most attractive and clever appeared at a local farmhouse appealing for food by using a casual and pleasant demeanor. Those with something to trade had an easier time of it. I was at my most charming when I went out to the nearby farms for food. Aunt Betty gave up several sets of bracelets, earrings and pins, which I bartered at an inflated rate of exchange. I seldom came back empty-handed, but the distance I had to cover increased with the growing shortages. The lack of ration stamps with my name on them meant less for Betty and the children.

✤ ✤ ✤

By the beginning of 1944, having the "secret" radio, the relief from bombing, and the nearness of her sister at the convent appeared to a calming influence on Aunt Betty. Less tense, she was ready to turn her attention to a variety of solutions where I was concerned. She had long discussions with Sister Agnella. Together they had come to an agreement. I should get back to my schooling. Agnella's convent experience and her well-established sense of pride served to root out the name of the nearest Gymnasium in Bamberg. Getting there proved to be the bigger problem. Having me go to live permanently on my grandfather's farm was out of the question; it was too far from a train station. Attendance at the Bamberg Gymnasium seemed impossible until other family members provided a solution. I would go and stay at a cousin's house in Stafflebach. There, I could take a train back and forth to the city. Most of the teachers at the Bamberg school were nuns. The only record I would need for registering was Sister Agnella's recommendation. Careful not to sound "defeated," both of my aunts used the growing unrest in the Rhineland to explain my late registration, and I began to attack pre-Algebra as it was practiced in Bavaria.

The "girls" in Stafflebach, Rosa and Greta were hardly young innocents. Mature, married women, they were sisters who were living together because their husbands were away in the army. Neither were they exactly my "cousins," a term we seemed to reserve for relatives with some family connection, perhaps long forgotten, but "family" nonetheless. What they presented for their young, new household member was a practical answer to my current needs. The women shared a house in a town with a railroad stop. The morning and afternoon trains would provide a time frame for a full day of schooling. Whatever arrangements were made, I was once again on the move, adjusting, readjusting with little thought of objecting. I had become very adept at being flexible. I was ready to go.

In the Bronx, my mother knew more about the progress of the war than she genuinely *wanted* to know. She had let herself believe that the newsreels in her local theater could make up for the lack of personal mail and communications of any kind from abroad. She tried her best to immerse herself in what she saw, but could merely wring her hands as she viewed images of bombs being dropped from far above the cities she knew were possible living areas for me. The bombing of factories in the Rhineland had disturbed her the most. She no longer knew what to say.

"What do you hear about the little one? Where is Sylvia?" one customer kept asking. He was one of the regulars, George, a bus driver from the near-by terminal.

Other interested friends suggested that mother might consider filing her own appeal for citizenship to add depth to her requests for news of her child's whereabouts. In July of 1944, nearly one month after the Allies landed on the beaches of Normandy in France, she received notification of becoming an official naturalized citizen. She then had engaged an attorney, who she hoped might at least assist her in her search for me. His expectations were not high. He knew that United States government lists didn't provide names of civilians, but he had contacts with other sources and helped in an appeal to the Red Cross, and every other known relief agency to see if I had been recorded anywhere as a fatality.

In the meantime, mother's customers and vendors refused to give up, and made additional contributions. With every major Allied campaign, the jar filled with change and had to be emptied out often. The invasion of France and other victories signaled anew the possibility of a "rescue," and the Hagopian brothers steadfastly fixed their thoughts on my safe return. They had a fund of their own. Although they never met with my mother socially, the brothers maintained their steadfast allegiance and literally kept her afloat financially. The smaller contributions in the jar gave her added emotional support. She left the jar where it was, a symbol of generosity and hope.

In the two years since she had received any news; the "Sylvia fund" grew. Stalwart in this regard, mother, still never used any of it to pay her own bills. Instead, she asked for prayers and said her own. "Wherever you are, Liebchen," she prayed at night, wanting to believe that I was still alive, but never knowing, "keep yourself safe!" For her part, she kept on going to the movies.

———

CHAPTER TWENTY-ONE

Down on the Farm

THERE WOULD BE an opportunity to go out to Trundstadt and my grandparent's farm before the school term wound its way toward the summer vacation. Walking along the dirt path, I tried to call up images of that first visit to the farm when the European trip had begun five years before. Uncle Walter and Aunt Betty and I had walked this way, crossed the river on a hand-pulled ferry, and walked some more. On the late spring day, five years later, I had followed Agnella's suggestion and made my way for a weekend respite from the Stafflebach home. From there, the farm could be reached in a half day of walking. Confident that my adult, female cousins could use a break from me as well, I knew the farm offered an entirely new experience—and a better food supply. Deep in the country, the war, the Bronx, all seemed at an improbable distance.

My memories hadn't included coming upon a cluster of farm houses; I'd pictured a more typical New York farm that included great stretches of pasture and a single house under several trees. This looked nothing like even the most modest upstate farm. My grandparents' house was among others in a circle around a central heap, a twenty-foot pile of rotting garbage, plant life and human wastes oozing into a dark pond of fluid emitting the worst smell imaginable. A month or so later, I would spend the entire summer there, and not be affected the same way by the odors; but some things you never get used to!

✡ ✡ ✡

My room was less a room and more a space under a roof connecting the house and a structured area for small farm animals. There was a variety of sounds I would later connect to a cow, chickens, rabbits and even a pig just on the other side of slatted wooden wall. I could hear them snuffling, squealing and scratching even at night. My bedding was nothing like the other grandparents' eiderdown; here, coarse muslin was stuffed with bits and pieces of what I swore were chicken feathers that invariably found their way close to the surface, making marks on my skin and further disturbing my sleep.

The shed noises woke me before the rising sun. I would have welcomed the light, anything that might have encouraged me to leave my skimpy coverlet. I conjured up the comfort offered by feathers taken from the soft underbelly of geese, but these stalks and thick shafts demanded my attention. I had set myself a goal of removing entire feathers that poked out through the muslin—until I worried that I might empty the cover entirely. I tried, I really *tried* just to be accommodating, but it was there in that bedding that I knew I would have to do something for myself. I made the first decision to change where I slept. Knowing that an upstairs bedroom, one I had seen but not been assigned had once been my father's, I eased myself away from the sounds of the animals and snuck up to the vacant bed upstairs. Early in the morning, undiscovered, I would scramble down to the place I had been assigned, and wait for the hissing, mooing and clucking to raise my grandparents at dawn.

On first weekend re-visit, there had been odd snatches of conversation about people living on the other side of the house, but that summer, unwilling to leave the comfort of the upstairs bed, and not wanting to be discovered, I was glad enough to hear that my father's brother, his wife and "some" children would not be among those who could discover my penchant for wandering at night. For some reason, these family members were not speaking to one another. I would have to wait for any explanation of the *dis*connection that kept the "ghost family" from sharing breakfast, the children from being potential playmates or the uncle from the work crew in the fields. None of them was ever introduced to me. When I was informed that I would spend my entire summer on the Trundtstatd farm, I had already learned *to pretend* to do what I had been told.

Life settled into a round of full days and restless nights creeping up and down stairs and counting on my internal clock to raise me up before dawn and the rooster's alarm. Though much quieter than my shed, the upstairs still creaked and groaned under foot. Still, there was no interaction with the "others." If no one wanted me to know what was going on, I wasn't going to ask.

Because we had so much of it, I tried introducing my grandmother to the American concept of eating corn at the table. I really hoped for a German version of corn on the cob. Water and ingredients perked and boiled for longer than I might have hoped, but the outcome was a tough version of kernels of paste that never changed into anything we could eat.

"Pig food," my grandmother huffed, and it was condemned. So much for my contribution. Instead I was given a series of jobs that included herding the ducks to water beyond the houses and the sickening garbage heap. I accepted a smooth stick to encourage feather donators in one direction or another. The ducks appeared to be as thrilled as I was to head away from their residence, but I worked harder trying to convince them to return. I whistled and hooted and tried a variety of sounds of encouragement when it was time to bring them back. They were reluctant to get out of the water, and as the weather turned hotter, I joined them in it.

☆ ☆ ☆

"You are not supposed to." A child's voice had called

"I am taking care of the ducks. They need to be in the water and I need to be with them." I responded, firmly.

A small boy and three girls appeared from behind a strand of trees at the water's edge. It seemed forever since I had been in the company of a group of children that weren't studying.

"We don't go in the water with our ducks."

"Have you been told not to?"

"No, but everyone knows the water is for them and not for us!"

"I can swim." I announced proudly to the boy. "Can you? Can they?" The biggest of the giggling girls nodded, no.

"Well if you can't swim, you can take off your shoes, put them next to mine and you can walk in and stay near the shore. I've been swimming many times." I paddled around in a circle, looking out at the nearby shore. I was surprised by the memory of my Mama's face as it flashed before me—my beautiful mother in the "latest" swim suit. I put my feet down and stood up in the pond water. It only came to my waist. "See, it's not deep and it is so cool. I have to get out now because I take the lunch to the men in the fields. I will be coming back tomorrow."

"Can we go in the water with you?"

"If you want to."

I let my mother's image fade. At least I had young friends to play with.

✠ ✠ ✠

I maintained my bedroom visitation as though I were the only child in the house. There was a minor reference made to the other uncle's family—and "the wife," but otherwise, I came to view the entire group in my imagination. I never knew what the trouble was, or if I did, I don't recall ever meeting them or learning what kept them apart.

By the middle of the summer, practically sure that I had successfully anticipated any and all interruptions of my routine upstairs, I wasn't prepared for the night a heavy weight of clothing was dropped on top of me, pressing brass buttons into my mouth and muting the sounds rising in my throat. I struggled to separate myself from the heap I thought must have been soaked in beer just before being hurled onto the bed. Using the convent method I'd developed to get myself out from tight covering, I inched sideways, until I actually fell off the side of the bed. Sucking in the cool night air, I thought about making my escape.

The idea of running across the room and down the stairs had quickly been negated by the swearing and questioning coming from the top of the bundle.

"What the hell?"

The clothing was alive; I'd heard that voice before.

"Papa?"

✷ ✷ ✷

The next morning, we had both managed to show up together at the breakfast table.

"How long will you be here?" Grandmother Rebhan, always practical and usually silent, asked the question, glaring when I interrupted telling my father, "You certainly surprised me..."

"I surprised myself," he smiled thinking about his trip across the fields. "I had to work hard not to fall off the ferry when crossing the river. I was congratulating myself when I thought I'd actually found my way into my own bed. I had no idea you would be in it."

I thought I might have done better with my grandmother if my father hadn't shared this bedroom occupancy on my part. His answer to his mother was short.

"My leave is up in two weeks. What's the matter, Mother? Ready to get rid of me already?"

She thumped a spoonful of thick oatmeal on a plate in front of her son. She was more than glad to see him, but she said, "Your father could use some help."

✡ ✡ ✡

It was a simple as that. No explanations further than his joining the men in the fields. There was no talk of the war; none of Mama or America.

Sitting high on the board placed across the sides of the cart, I held on to the harness reins that stretched across the back of the animal assigned to do the pulling. It was a cow.

"I brought the lunches today. The cow knew the way." I noted as I pulled the cart close to the group of men expecting lunch and the cool drink I'd been sent to deliver. I sat over a large container of beer. My father spied the can. "Ah, and she's brought us the best beer in the world!" He lifted the can out. In a minute, he had it open and had spooned a ladle full into his mouth. The second spoonful he offered to me. I drank it.

"Good, ja?"

I managed to avoid my grandfather's look of disapproval. I knew I wasn't really breaking the rules; I'd already been told that having made my Confirmation in my faith, I was entitled to have beer with the adults at meals. But cold beer out of a ladle in the fields was so much better than the thin cow's milk I'd been given, knowing the best creamy part had been drawn off to make butter. I ate my lunch, and drank my beer with my father. For his part, he spent his days in the fields and most nights drinking at a distance with friends.

I think he was mostly drunk every night and fell into the bed I kept warm until he managed his way up to his room. I moved down to sleep at the bottom as would a family puppy. In all that time, he never explained how he had come to live in Germany without my mother. But, he was, after all, my father, and I was sorry to see him go back to his unit although he spent every evening "out." It would be more than two years before he reappeared, once again under very different "circumstances."

Of all those lives I seemed to be living, in the long run I loved the farm. My work load was far less demanding than running the household with or for Aunt Betty. It was peaceful and gentle out there playing with the ducks, splashing in the water with the neighborhood children. Some times I went to the small dry goods store my grandmother stocked. She trusted me to sell and measure out the variety of items, flour and canned goods, and let me handle the money. Of course, when "driving," holding onto the reins atop the cart, I imagined I was the great rancher going off into some version of wonderland with that old cow, or I became the princess following the golden goose, gathering eggs laid here and there by uncooperative hens—everything else faded.

There were times, though, in the early mornings next to the noisy animals when my mind would wander. Just before my 12th birthday that September, and the beginning of the next school term, I would find myself in yet another world, allowing the luxury of thinking ahead, projecting into the future—or worse, engaged in some sort of reverie from my past. I suffered the universal disorder of the displaced, and was *still* homesick. I had tried to avoid such thinking for when I did reminisce, I still had memories of—and missed—my mother. There was one big change; I no longer cried.

———

CHAPTER TWENTY-TWO

Learning the Hard Way

THE TRAIN HAD been late—again. It was the third time in two weeks before my birthday that I had to stand on the platform holding an armload of books grown heavier with time. The assorted would-be-passengers had begun murmuring a litany of reasons—primary among them was the current dismay. The war was going badly for the Fatherland. There had been reports of Allied incursions into Germany itself—and the Russian front had moved westward. I tried not to think about what it meant to me. All I had to do was to get myself to school and then make some plan for supper with the girls in Stafflebach. I started counting how many times I could sway from one foot to another. I was up to fifteen when I saw the engine approaching. Finally, I climbed aboard the train.

Ordinarily I might have used the time it took to get to my school station stop to read an assignment or make a note or two in my thin, but well used notebook. This day was not ordinary. I don't remember why I chose to look out the train window—to follow the path of what I imagined was a hawk circling above a distant field, or why I felt compelled to point it out to my seat mate, an older man with a big leather brief-case in his lap. We watched together as the "bird" appeared to find its prey and dive through the early morning mist. The man began to rock back and forth in his seat, struggling to raise himself above it before landing on his feet.

"Airplane!" he screamed, "enemy airplane!" He pitched forward with the sudden motion of brakes being applied; the engineers had seen *it,* too, and were stopping the train. He began to shout at me. "Get out! We have to get out!" He was pulling on my arm. "Leave the books; leave them—we must get to the door!"

In less than two minutes I heard and felt the effects of the attack. Metal scraped against metal, sounding a further alarm. Passengers joined a chorus of screeching, punctuated by a drumbeat of bullets splattering along of the forward cars and biting into the earth on either side of the train. People tumbled out even as the train was not yet at a full stop. Shoved out the door by people behind me, I leapt over a pair of legs gone sideways and began to run down the embankment built up for the tracks. Uncertain of the best route to safety, I ran instinctively at a right angle into the open field, driven by a need to create a distance between myself and the tracks. I passed several passengers who had chosen to throw themselves to the ground, their hands raised up to cover their heads; I briefly considered doing the same thing but my feet appeared to have settled into a motion of their own, and I allowed them to carry me further away.

I could see a clump of trees in the distance at the edge of the corn rows. I changed my direction and headed toward them, never stopping until I could throw myself into the raised root section of the largest tree in a line. I ducked down and waited for—something, I didn't know what. I just knew I should stay there—and hope. My heart was pumping so much blood in my ears; I couldn't be certain that there were any other sounds filtering across the field. The plane had gone from view. What was that? Was it over? A few heads appeared above the grassy distance and soon enough there were several people moving back toward the tracks. Still charged up by my own adrenalin, I thought perhaps I ought to do the same, that I had a big distance to cover. And then I saw them—three of them running toward me. The woman was holding a huge pocketbook between her waist and her chin. Moving with it caused her to rock as much from side to side as it did to move her forward. I stood up, and when the woman saw me, she yelled, "Get down, get down! It's coming back! They always come back!"

By the time the scramblers reached the trees and tumbled into the hollow, I knew *she* had been right. The *hawk* appeared once again. We were at least a hundred yards from the train, but the sound of diving engines and thudding bullets pushed all three of us into a constricting embrace. The children covered their ears and tucked their heads under the woman's skirt as the ducks had done with their mamas one rainy day on the farm.

✫ ✫ ✫

In the Bronx, my mother shifted in her seat. The MovieTone Newsreels flickered on the screen above her. She had come after finishing up at the bakery. She was late—the available seats were well up front. She had to tilt her head back and lift her eyes to watch. She had missed the first movie in the double feature presentation. She wasn't disappointed since she knew she was in time for the up-dated news shown between pictures.

Allied troops were marching above her. There were several scenes of the progress made since they had crossed the English Channel and landed in France. "D" Day had been played and replayed. *Soon*, they would approach Germany. Over and over, she watched images of mass destruction that followed; cities in ruins flooded the screen. The casualties reached into hundred of thousands, into the millions.

For more than four years, my mother had grieved for all of them, soldiers and civilians alike. Yet, all that time, through every newsreel, she held out hope for her family, confident that Walter would have thought of a way to elude the greatest threats and get to what she believed was safety in the east, to Agnella, to the hills, somewhere far from harm. She had counted on that. She was still counting on it until that one evening when she saw the pictures taken by British pilots. There was a whole series of grainy images from cameras imbedded in the noses of planes that attacked anything that moved on German roads and rails. Allied aircraft were deep into Germany, into the countryside; she identified the hills of Bavaria. My mother shuddered. "Sylvia," she screamed out loud, with such terror that no one shushed her.

Above the train, the plane had made a looping circle in the sky and was approaching for a third pass. There was no doubt in my mind. The target appeared to be the still-puffing train engine. Not everyone in the field agreed with my assessment. Fearing the strafing would include them, those who could, rose as one after the plane passed beyond them. From the distance, strung out in a line, they looked like fence posts on the move as they tried to get farther and farther away from the train, lessening, they hoped, their chances of being hit by the splattering bullets. After a fourth pass, a direct hit pierced the train engine and it exploded. The fireball punched through the sky sending glowing bits of metal into the field where anguished screams added to the echoes rolling toward the tree line. After a few attempts to put out threatening fires in the grass, no one moved.

In a painful few minutes, my companion in the trees released her grip. Having reached what appeared to be the end of her own terror, she sat up and began to wipe at the children's faces, first spitting on a fold in her skirt. She reassured them, murmuring a language I had not ever heard before. The children sat up, leaning against her as the woman rummaged through her bag. Her arm went in up to her elbow as she stirred the contents until she withdrew a large, round compact, opened it and held it in one hand to look into the side with its embedded mirror. Using her other hand, a thumb and two fingers, she withdrew a fitted powder puff with which she first made several circular swipes on the cake of powder in the other half. She wiped under her eyes and patted her cheeks and the bridge of her nose, and rubbed it across her forehead before replacing it. She made all sorts of wheezing sounds before withdrawing a lipstick that she opened to make a blood red circle in the middle of her pursed lips. I watched, fascinated by the ritual. It had been years since I saw a female putting on any make-up—and misusing it in such a manner. With one last look at her reflection, the woman clicked her compact shut and dropped it and the lipstick back into the deep recesses of her bag. She was ready to talk to me—in German.

"In Russia, they killed the trains and the *peoples*," she said, her German halting and drenched in a heavy accent. "You are too young to know this horror, this killing of peoples by their own peoples. This is my third war." I paid attention.

We spent most of the day together after the train was 'killed;' she told me *her* story. She was a *White* Russian, an aristocrat from a family that had been close enough to royalty and the Czar to be forced to leave Russia after the revolution there in what proved to be the middle of World War I. Thousands had been killed in the Russian fighting that raged between the *Reds*, the Communists, and the *Whites*, anyone really who the Reds thought were the opposition. She fled with other Whites. On that trip across the Steppes in eastern Poland; she had been on a train that came under an attack. Planes with two wings were dropping bombs and firing machine guns. That war had started on horse back. Terror from the skies had been added to the combat. Few had survived. She became a "refugee," a wanderer in search of safety. She told me that she had no papers to present to German authorities and could not leave even though she was allowed to stay because she represented a universal European concept of "Noblesse oblige," the idea that "royalty" deserved some special treatment. She had lived with friends at first, using some of her jewelry to cover her living expenses. She showed a special group of pockets high on the inside of her skirt, a place where separate precious stones could be hidden. It was a method used by people who were used to having their land over-run, their homes confiscated. I soon realized that she showed me these hiding places because they were empty.

She had met and married another Russian, and had borne the two children she had with her. They never spoke. Instead, they nestled against their mother and closed their eyes; they had heard the tale before. Her husband had thought to take them all back to their homeland, but that option disappeared with the first German accord with the Russian government; then there had been the declaration of war between the Nazis and the Communists. She lowered her voice to say, "He went to a meeting of Russians still hoping for a return of a government loyal to the monarchy. We have not seen him since. Like everything I have ever loved, I am afraid he has been reduced to rubble."

She asked about me, why I had been on the train. I told her about school and my "cousins." I told her about Aunt Betty, and Horst and Ingeborg. I even told her about Uncle Walter and his required service in the German army. I knew it was all right to tell her everything.

"I am an American," I blurted out.

"You lucky girl," she said, hugging me. "I am so happy for you. You will have a home to go to when this madness is over."

I wanted to believe her. I started to allow myself the thought. I wanted to get back home. Even more, I wanted to go back to the train and get my meager lunch packet. I had assured myself that I would starve to death first.

———

CHAPTER TWENTY-THREE

The Vise

THE COUSINS LISTENED to my harrowing ordeal, and the sad tale of the Russian lady nodding and clucking knowingly as neither of them knew what had happened to their own husbands. I added that the wanderer and her children had disappeared into a different train section after an engineer signaled an all clear. Once the rest of the passengers were sure of themselves, they all returned to the cars and we were told we would have to wait for a new engine. It seemed that those who had scrambled aboard first had already searched through the hastily discarded belongings. I would have lost my lunch that day, had it not been hidden out-of-sight thanks to my seat mate's briefcase, which had been opened and searched, but remained on top of my food.

No doubt about it; sooner or later the entire railroad system would be affected by the strafing. I really had no other means of getting back to Adelsdorf, and there was still the prospect of going north for Christmas. I would have to take a train or not be able to have my traditional orange and cookies with Aunt Betty and the children. By this time, I was content to know that the holiday would be, at the very least, celebrated at the convent. I didn't think I could manage without the lights, the garlands and the singing, even though I had no expectations of chocolate. With an honest concern for my safety, I took the available trains both ways, and tried not to look out the window.

Christmas brought its own memories—revisited. The Adelsdorf living quarters were enhanced with a "real" tree adorned with real candles. Of course, there were no stockings filled with oranges; there had been a few cookies courtesy of Mrs. Been in the bakery below. Meager but meaningful; we had settled on that concept. We had no "real" comprehension of the idea that this Christmas would be the last of its kind for all of us.

Soon after the holiday, I knew I would have to find an alternate route to school. The trains were under attack every day, if there was one to be had. The Stafflebach cellar held an answer. I could use an old bike we found among the discarded household goods. We cleaned it up, pumping fresh air into the tires and oiling the chain. That winter, I pedaled to school through all kinds of weather. I don't think I caught cold or got sick, but I was always more than ready to get into bed early and stay in. My routine was changing in every way. I was beginning to feel threatened. Until then, the *country, the German people* had been *at* war. Then, it seemed, the war had come to Bavaria—*to* me.

Little did I know I was in training for the bike ride of my life.

☆ ☆ ☆

Aunt Betty was positive. For two months she had struggled against the inevitable. For years she had told anyone who would listen that she suffered from "heart troubles," although what they were, in particular, no one knew. I considered them in terms of my Aunt's refusal to work hard or long at lifting or taking on household responsibilities. I didn't believe that such infirmity would actually take my aunt's life, but Betty had come to believe her own dire projections.

Far from her doom and gloom, I had reached a point where I knew I was enduring a different form of chaos. I was living in the war, just hoping to get through what ever it was and would come to be. I was doing my best to act as if I were getting a regular education in an irregular situation. Everyone in my classes had a personal story of the war's escalation.

It was real. Everything I learned was from what I heard in fleeting conversations among school girls and my Stafflebach neighbors.

Most people were fully pressed under the weight of what it would mean to have the enemy soldiers come to them. To the west, the Rhine had been crossed by the English, the French and the Americans. In the east, the Russians had endured the siege of Stalingrad and were moving west. Having lived through the bombings and the strafing from the sky above me, I knew I was going to have to face war on the ground. Then I heard about the tanks—and the flamethrowers!

Having heard descriptions of these mechanized armored bugs, I still had no genuine comprehension of the destruction they could bring to bear Truly, my interest was as peaked as it had been behind Frau Eigen's house where I had come upon the most grotesque of bugs, including a praying mantis, pinching and piercing them and dispatching the ugliest. However, when I was told more about these mammoth steel and iron vehicles, school children's tales included sounds that would "tear your ears off." These beasts could roll over trucks and piles of concrete with their wheels on rotating tracks; their guns could bring down a building. There was no stopping them, and they were rolling over the Bavarian countryside. Worse, the flamethrowers shot balls of fire, burning everything at a distance. I tried not to think about what it was like to be burned; it was a pain I knew. If all this destruction was coming our way, I actually prayed that they would go around Stafflebach, or to the best possible target—pass us up altogether, drive over to Bamberg and bring down the school building.

☆ ☆ ☆

Aunt Betty was so desperate, she had retrieved and cleaned the radio on her own. She sat with it close to her ear to mute the sound. For Germans, the news was not good. The Italians had been over run, the Rhine River had been crossed, and except for one frenzied, late moment of glory in a major surprise counter attack to the north, the German army was basically fighting from a fallback position. The Allies were moving east across Germany. The day-time voice of Hitler split the airways with the diatribes laced with his continuous "super weapon" threat. But Betty, still holding on to a semblance of her practical nature, knew that if the German troops were retreating east through Adelsdorf, the American's would follow. There would be a battle.

She had heard stories of resistance from German civilians. Not far from Adelsdorf, locals had pounded American forces and done their best to thwart the Allies' forward progress. True to her nature, my aunt had recoiled from the stories of the Russians coming in—raping and pillaging being among her deepest fears. There above the bakery, with her two children, she concluded that her family was going to be squeezed in the space between German enemies.

She made one last visit to the convent to pray with her sister.

"Men can win or lose in war, and go on to the next one," Sister Agnella had said, "but, in war, women and children always lose."

For Betty, even the convent wasn't safe; she had one option—to run and hide. She sent for me.

✡ ✡ ✡

Artillery bursts peppered the distant hills turning night into a false dawn beyond the ridgelines. Miles away, I looked out the second story window, each of the girls squeezed into the frame on either side. From this vantage point, we could more than imagine the battles that seemed perched and poised to roll down the distant hills.

I saw the approaching figure, first. Somebody was pumping the pedals of a bike, standing over the chain wheel and racing in our direction. Alerted by my poke in the ribs, Greta and Rosa watched the rider speed into the front yard and stop by turning into the loose gravel.

"Hey up there."

We jumped in unison and breathed a common sigh of relief having identified the voice of a young woman.

"Does Sylvia Rebhan live here?"

Rosa answered for all three of us. "Who wants to know?"

The answer came swiftly. "My name is Annaliese; I have to talk to her. I have a message from Adelsdorf, from her Aunt Betty."

I could hardly believe it. I called out, "I'm Sylvia, and you came all the way from Adelsdorf...on that bike...just to give me a message?"

"Actually, I've come to take you back with me," she added.

The idea of going all that way—with a stranger, certainly didn't appeal to me. Instead, fearing some bad news about the children, Horst and Ingeborg, I asked for the message. She looked straight up at me and said calmly, "Your aunt said to tell you, 'We are all going to die.'"

"That's it?" I yelled down into the yard. "You rode all this way to tell me my aunt thinks we are all going to die?"

"Yes, but that's not the whole message. She said to tell you, 'Since you are all going to die, you should come back to Adelsdorf so you can die, *together.*'"

I knew she had come from Betty. Considering the source, the message made perfect sense.

———

CHAPTER TWENTY-FOUR

You Can't Get There From Here

STILL FULLY DRESSED as she had been against the early spring frost, Annaliese had fallen into a deep sleep on a couch in the front room on the first floor, a long, skinny but muscular leg hanging over the end of a horsehair stuffed arm. She was extremely thin, but so were we all. I hadn't made any connection at first. I wondered if it was at all possible—if I had known her from those first town school days when I lived at the convent. Whoever she was, Betty had sent her and I had agreed to go. I had the distinct feeling that my messenger was guarding the front door against any change of heart on my part. As it was, we started out together on our bikes as the genuine dawn rose to join the orange of the battles' distant firestorm.

My meager wardrobe, all my belongings in fact, were packed in a large box tied to a rack on the fender of the rear wheel of my bike. The contents contained a hair brush, two handkerchiefs, two pair of panties, a pair of socks, a dress, one skirt, a short sleeved sweater and a blouse—and the little sixth birthday autograph book I had brought with me on the Bremen. I was wearing my only pair of shoes, woolen stockings held up by clips attached to my underwear, a skirt, blouse, sweater and my newly altered winter coat. I left all my notebooks and papers behind, except for my precious copy of my birth certificate, which I had carefully sewn between the lining and the outer cloth of my coat.

I had learned something about carrying precious items from the Russian lady under the trees.

My companion/guide/leader had nothing to say until we had pedaled well out of Stafflebach. Annaliese knew the way. She took us out of town, having used the railway crossing to follow a gravel-packed dirt path adjacent to the tracks. The early morning air hung heavy with the aroma of pine trees weighed down with a light frost.

"Pedaling will keep us warm, you'll see. Making this accommodation is the easy part. Our difficult times will come as we cross battle lines. They have surely changed since I rode out to you."

"Won't the soldiers stop us?"

"Not if we do this right. As long as we look pur-poseful and focus on the ground straight ahead, they will be too busy to notice. We just have to look as though we belong. I'll do all the talking."

She didn't have to tell me. Along with learning to read German, I had been schooled in the art of reactive behavior. The idea was *not* to talk, *not* to look as though you had anything to say, and *not* to do anything that could be noticed or misconstrued as something you *might* want to say. I had come to the conclusion early that under this dictatorship, which turned out to be as hard on the German civilians as it had been on its enemy aliens, I would have to take my cues from the adults around me. Unlike my American relatives, these people had taught me to be as gray as the German sky.

✡ ✡ ✡

"They've been here." Annaliese raised one hand to signal. "We can't go through this way."

We had come around a small embankment that had kept us from seeing the death and dying of the land beyond. Stretched out before us were the carcasses of trees and bushes that had been reduced to withered black strands perched on the edge of deep holes. Shattered tree trunks blinked with live embers. Smoke curled up from pine needles packed into unfamiliar shapes. What wasn't hot—wasn't—there. Nearby were mounds of earth that hadn't seen the light of day for hundreds of years.

"The heat will melt our tires," the ever practical Annaliese had warned.

We could still feel the effects of battle in the air we began to breathe. It was thick and sweet with gun powder. What had been pristine and green crackled with burnt remnants. Black, twisted stumps oozed boiling tar. There was a slight change in the wind filling our noses and eyes with acrid and dank air that made us choke. The entire broken field began to hiss. It had started to rain.

"Won't the rain help?" I hoped.

"Not enough. We'll have to go around. This way!" She picked up her bike, turned it and began to pedal toward a distant patch of green. "We'll have to go faster if we want to get to Adelsdorf before they do."

Neither of us knew which who "they" would be. Even if the destroyers of a once beautiful forest had been Americans, I can honestly say I wouldn't have tried to approach them. Annaliese; was a teenager away from her home, and I was just trained to be a follower of the first order and obedient beyond meas- ure. It was my job to go with this girl and get back to Aunt Betty and the children. To do that, I was going to face a variety of men who might do us both some harm if we were discovered and considered anything other than local children, passing through. Silence was my choice. I had survived so far by keeping my head down, which I did again—and I pedaled.

Late in the afternoon, the rain intensified. Some of the dirt roadway we had been using filled with wide puddles, and we had to get off and walk our bikes through the deep ruts. There was no mistaking the "foot prints"—they were tank tracks.

"We have to ride faster, now!" said Annaliese. We were about to pass a group of soldiers hunched under their ponchos. One of them called out, in German. "Look at the two little ducks who don't know enough to get out of the rain. Come over here!"

Annaliese answered brightly, "Oh no! We can't stop. We are on our way home from school and we can't delay—or our mama will beat us with a stick!"

The soldiers laughed. All of them could identify with an angry parent's punishment; some shifted the weapons they were carrying to wave us past them on the road. I could only hope they would consider my shivering as a reaction to the weather and not to them. We increased our speed and rode our fastest until the soldiers were out of sight.

Without notice, my legs would not work. I fell off both pedals and stumbled forward. "I can't make my knees bend."

Annaliese stopped. "Yes, I know. Stand still for a minute, and then we will walk."

Unsure of moving anything below my waist, I couldn't move. I had built my strength riding all those miles to school, but this cramping was beyond painful. My companion came back reaching out to steady my bike. "Now, lift your leg over the chain, that's it, now left, right, left, right. See you are moving. We will just go across this field and up a small hill. I passed an empty barn on my way. You'll be able to sleep. Come now."

I don't remember much of anything else from that first night on the road, except that in spite of my pain, I was able to move to the shed when I could see it. Annaliese told me in the morning that she had led me to a dry area where some ancient left-over hay served as our bed.

Whatever strength, whatever internal capacity to see this period of my life as another adventurous expedition and not a dangerous one, that same attitude seemed to be sapping my physical reserve—a growing awareness, and the ever present hunger. When I woke, I had my face pressed into Annaliese's coat. I lifted her head, spoke into her face and claimed, "I can smell cheese." Annaliese stuffed her hand into both her pockets and pulled out two small packets. Peeling away the paper wraps from a bit of bread in one, and cheese in the other, she protested. "I swear I didn't put these here. If I had known they were there, I might have eaten them on the way."

We knew who did it. *She* certainly couldn't have us die of hunger before reaching her—so we could die together. We actually laughed and said in unison, "Aunt Betty."

———

CHAPTER TWENTY-FIVE

Home Again, Home Again, Lickety Split

TANK TRACKS AND more tank tracks. We maneuvered our bikes over and around them, bumping along other troughs etched in mud by marching feet. Just outside of Adelsdorf, we came upon the makers of the footprints—more German soldiers, several of whom were digging at the muddy earth with small shovels.

"Mine fields," said Annaliese. "They are planting mines." (How she accumulated this knowledge I never knew.) "Those things blow up if you step on them. Good thing we didn't ride over any of those."

I had to agree.

In the main portion of the road in front of the church, there were a few more soldiers—digging. We rode right past them, avoiding the growing piles next to their holes. Even I knew from my Rhineland games that these men were going to half-bury themselves in their personal trenches—to fight.

✫ ✫ ✫

In my absence, Betty had prepared for my arrival, confident that because she had needed it to happen, it would. She had an escape plan, having found (or at least appropriated) a two-wheeled cart, which she had piled high. In a matter of days after Annaliese delivered me as promised, Betty had put her plan into action. She had packed the cart with clothing and bedding—and then would add the two children. She was ready to go.

Betty had contained herself as long as she could before offering me another of her high pitched commands:

"Hurry! Come help me. We have to go, now! The tanks are coming and they are going to fight right here! Hurry, hurry, hurry!"

She was the worst I had ever seen her. The children seemed frozen in their nest; I can't remember if Horst had anything to say. I had my back to him soon enough and grabbed at the free handle of the cart.

"Pull," she screamed, "Pull" and she started off with a sort of trot. We had traveled a hundred yards before coming upon a collection of townspeople, mostly women, several children and old man or two moving away from the village with a steady purpose.

"Wait." Betty stopped! The result was an uneven transfer of weight that ripped the handle out of my grip. I saved Ingeborg from toppling to the ground. Horst had managed to steady himself by holding onto one of the cart's side rails.

"I forgot! You have to go back!" Betty lifted the cart to make it level and set her foot against one wheel to keep it still.

I was astonished. "Back?" I couldn't believe what I was hearing.

"Yes. Back to the grocery store!"

What could possibly be of such value that I had to go back? I thought, but didn't ask. I didn't want to delay her answer.

"She promised me...and I paid for it. You have to go back."

I turned to move. I felt like the last runner in a relay race, just anxious for the passing of the baton.

"What am I getting?" I was screaming above the noise. Guns were being fired at a distance. The air was filling with smoke and I could hear men shouting. "What am I getting?" I called back over my shoulder.

"My jelly." She was actually saying, "jelly," and she had a *reason*. In all that chaos, she had a *reason.*

"This may be our one chance to get it. She promised me!"

I bolted forward. The noises began to surround me, but I kept on running. I cut a zigzag path around and through the fox holes, each of them filled with men whose eyes I could see beneath their helmets, the end of their guns resting on the mound of dirt that encircled their trenches. Some of those eyes were watching me dart first here and then there, like the geese again. Past the bakery, past the church. I could see the store front beyond the last two foxholes. I thought one of the soldiers shouted out, but if he was saying that I should stop, I didn't hear him. And I knew I wouldn't stop, that I couldn't. I burst through the door. The woman who ran the grocery was standing in front of the counter, a jar of jelly in her outstretched hand. I took it.

"Run," she said, as though I needed to be told. "Run!"

✩ ✩ ✩

As difficult as it was to watch the newsreel (she had left her seat twice before it began) my mother remained transfixed. The main feature was over. The second movie, the traditional "B," black-and-white thriller was soon to begin. She had come to the theater with George, one of the bus drivers. He had long been a regular customer. Like others, he had been part of the city transport system with its terminal on Eighth Avenue. He began and ended his day eating his breakfast at one of her tables. One of the "good guys," he had begun a gentle courtship of the beautiful woman behind the counter. A widower, he lived with his former mother-in-law in a New York apartment. His son, a boy of 12, was in a private school run by the Irish Christian Brothers. He had managed to talk his way into mother's miniscule social life and insisted on going to the movies with her.

"You shouldn't watch this stuff by yourself."

In the end, she gave in. The man could "charm the birds out of their nests." She needed to sit next to someone she knew. She had taken to shouting out during the stories of the battles—and there were so many of them. But this week in particular, she was heartsick. She thought the news had been all—bad. Images of a sorrowful America filled every theater. President Roosevelt had died on April 12. This time, mother let her friend hold her hand.

"I'm afraid," she admitted.

"You're safe," he tried to say; "The war will be over soon. We have a feisty new President—Truman. The Americans are winning now."

"No," she dismissed him for not getting it. "I'm not afraid for *me*. I'm afraid for my Sylvia. It's the Germans. I know those people. I'm afraid they won't surrender until everyone over there is dead."

The Adelsdorf band of evacuees took refuge. We had a ready-made shelter in a three-story underground set of deep cellars, which had served as storage areas for a brewery. Pushing the cart into a ditch, Betty and some of the others clamored down the flights of

177

metal stairways, pushing their way through the iron doors separating the levels.

Not everyone went down with them right away. I was too short to see what was happening at a distance. While others sat above ground or went below, I instinctively climbed a wounded but standing tree. From my perch I could see into the hills far beyond Adelsdorf. Spilling over the crest was a column of German tanks and groups of infantry soldiers who hovered close to the vehicles as they came down the incline. The tanks rolled forward relentlessly. It seemed forever before they rattled through Adelsdorf, past the dug-in advance group, avoiding the men in the foxholes. They kept grinding forward, until they traversed a bridge into the fields beyond where Sister Agnella had made her crossing. There, they turned into a formation facing the village. More foot soldiers split into groups hovering behind or near the half circle.

I called down the sequence of events. After a huge explosion and several rising columns of smoke, I reported, "It looks like they've blown up the bridge." My announcement sent some of the remaining women down into the cellars. I stayed in my cat- bird's seat. It was fascinating! "Other soldiers are branching out to the fields near the dirt road—next to the church." I followed Annaliese's thinking. "Mines," I said. "They are planting more mines!" With that piece of information, more of my traveling defectors moved down the stairs.

It may have been less than an hour or more when I saw another set of tanks at the top of the hill—their profiles distinctly different—Americans making their way through the woods followed by their own Infantry men churning down at full speed. There was no mistaking the weapon of choice for an array of the Americans on foot. The sound reached across the miles. There was a series of brilliant fireballs reaching horizontally, setting trees and grass ablaze, each one followed by a roaring—whoosh.

"Flamethrowers!" I reported.

I lost my audience altogether. Even I thought better of it; yet, I stayed to watch the outnumbered German tanks turn and make a hasty retreat far to the left of the groups' hiding place.

"Rifle fire and machine guns," I added as I climbed down and jumped to the ground and banged through the doors pounding down the metal steps pushing through the second and third doorways past the big beer barrels stacked off to the side.

For years, I had been so detached from the reality of death under fire; at that time, *I* could have been watching my own life at the movies with my mother. But I had seen it, my first and what might be my last armored battle and I was finally—worried.

We all stayed put over night. As dark as it was in the cellar, we could see the light of dusk fade from between and through the cracks around the doors above. In the morning, there was no mistaking the sound of the American tanks when they rumbled closer to our hiding place. There was some nervous coughing and then silence. I could hear my own breath as I drew it in. Several children whimpered but were soon rocked or shushed to sleep. We were all mostly frozen in place by the sounds of battle, the crackle of rifles, the heavy thuds of larger guns, hours of bombardments, firing, and return firing, each with its own distinct part of the orchestration of destruction.

Then, a new silence. The audience in the cellar began to whisper opinions. After hours and hours of no close sounds echoing down the stairs, there were the newer sounds of tanks on the move. An old man offered, "Maybe they're going north…and east." Was that good? Where were they? The non-combatants in the cellar were fighting fear, hunger, and fatigue, and they wondered if they were at the edge of an attack—or in the thick of one.

✲ ✲ ✲

It seemed loud—forever. Then it was quiet. Was it over? Someone suggested staying still until the light pierced the dust and foul air. Then they would go up and see. More heavy gunfire. What ever was making those sounds was right above us. The noises were close to the entrance.

The upper-most set of double doors was flung open, iron banging itself on the stone walls and swinging back to the point of closing, until they were pushed open wide once more, their metal hinges protesting. There was shouting and the presence of enough daylight for us refugees to peer up around the frame of their third level hiding place. What we could see were two columns of shadows, men moving slowly down the stairs, guns at the ready, pointed bayonets—mounted.

I prayed—Please God, not the flamethrowers, not the flamethrowers!

The second set of hinges screamed out, grinding upon themselves in an ever- growing, eardrum-piercing announcement as the doors were shoved open by the advancing troops—soon applying more pressure on the metal steps.

Was God listening? Was there to be no other sound than the boots pressing downward?

There was the in-take of air through parched throats squeezed tight in terror. Soon enough, there was another eerie stillness.

I pressed myself backward into people already pushing against the casks that nearly filled the space on their own. There was no place to hide.

Utter silence. Then a lingering screech stabbed through the dark as the third level doors whined under pressure, scraping their bottom edges on the surface of dirt and stone. A few iron shavings caught in particles of light drifted to the floor! And next— light, brilliant light crashed in upon us.

I held my breath as long as I could, anticipating instant cremation. But there was no fire, no smell of burning fuel! I exhaled when able to fix the idea in my head; we had been caught in a series of probing flashlight beams.

"Well, well. What do we have here?" said a voice behind the yellow arc. "Come out, you mothers…! Come out of there!"

I was the one who moved—these were *my* Americans! This was it. Now or never! I ingested the knowledge like a full meal, chewed it and pulled it down into my core—and no flamethrowers.

I heard a voice—it was mine—an inner force that still had no sound. "Move forward," it said, "Move forward and tell him—tell them all—in ENGLISH!" But I could barely move, never mind talk.

With a feeble motion, I turned back the corner of my coat pulling at the threads that encased my precious paper. The nearest soldier holding his gun at the ready, said, "What the Hell?"

I was lifting my coat up.

"I'm not interested, kid." He misunderstood.

"Please," I remembered. "Please, look at this! Look at my paper. I am an American." Continuing in his direction, I snatched out my certificate.

"What the….?" he bellowed, lowering the weapon and grabbing me with his free hand. "Come here and lemme see that! Damn if you ain't!" He read. "You're—you *are* an American!" His training made him ask, "Who else is down here?"

"Old people…(Where did those words come from? I was amazed.)…just old and kinder—children, children."

"Are they Americans, too?"

"No," I said firmly, "but don't hurt them!" How much of that I said in decent English, I can't recall.

He swung the beam of his light over the group, the pathetic remainder of the battle for Adelsdorf.

"OK, kid. You are coming with me. I gotta show you to the Lieutenant before he sends down more guys. *This area's clear!*" he called up the stairs, and with that, in a one-handed lift, he swooped me up onto his shoulder. Instinctively I put an arm around his neck, not so much as to balance myself as to physically show my relief and faith even as I *needed* to hold on; and he turned and thudded up the steps between the astonished rows of soldiers.

Betty was screaming after me—in German. "Don't go with them, don't go! They'll rape you, they'll rape you!"

I held on, leaning my head next to his helmet, feeling the cool of its steel next to my burning cheek.

Whatever "rape" meant, I knew they wouldn't. "I am an American." I wrapped both arms around his neck and prepared myself to say it again and again. But more importantly, I had finally made my own decision to say what I had not dared to wish or hope for—for six long years! "—and I want to go home!"

———

CHAPTER TWENTY-SIX

G.I.'s

"SHE'S FROM THE Bronx," the Lieutenant announced to the soldiers nearer one of the tanks. "She says her mother lives on Clay Avenue." They cheered. "Somebody write that down. This little lady is one f—in' American." He apologized quickly. "Pardon my French," he said, "I mean, she's one beautiful American kid, and she wants to go home."

"So do we!" shouted one of the soldiers.

I wish I had asked every name, could even tell you who they said they were. I had to look it up, years later. One of them put me right up on the front of a tank and several stuffed chocolate bars in my hands. And they all smiled beautiful white, crescent-moon smiles on the dirtiest faces I had seen on men. As a matter of fact, there were more men surrounding me and the nearest tank than I had seen up close all year.

The chocolate wouldn't stay down. I leaned over and threw up, and they cheered again. "She ain't used to it," said one. "My kids do that if they eat too many sweets." One after another they pressed closer to look at the prize they had won by crossing the Rhine River into Germany. It was as though they had come just to get *me*. I was filled with a pride and a comfort I had not known before that day.

"My, oh my" said the Lieutenant having introduced me to everyone in his immediate command. "Now, Betty...is it?" he said handing me back my certificate. "We still have to go after the bad guys, so what are we going to do with you?"

I wanted them *all* to know. "My Mama calls me, *Sylvia*. I've been living with my aunt in Adelsdorf, over the bakery." I was amazed at the English words that came out of my mouth along with the chocolate. I tried not to throw up on anyone by leaning over the side of the tank.

"OK, Sergeant," he said as he pounded on the tank, "about-face this mother...sorry...and take this young lady back into that town."

I didn't understand all of what he was saying but they actually turned the tank around and drove it back into the village with me sitting on top at the right of its big gun. I couldn't help but notice that the tank drove right over several of the foxholes, some of which were plugged by the dead bodies of German soldiers. Mrs. Been had emerged from her cellar just in time to stare open-mouthed at my victory ride.

A voice crackled inside the tank. The driver was standing in the open hatch, swearing. "Sorry" he said to me while telling the others, "They've got incoming up in front of us. Hop down kid. We gotta go! You understand? We'll be back, and then we'll see what else we can do for *you*, Honey."

I could hardly believe that they had come. I couldn't have asked for more. They had already turned the tank back around to rumble out and join the others when I thought of it. I ran after them shouting. "America, tell America...tell my mother you found Sylvia—please!"

It was several hours before I saw Betty and the children making their way toward the house. Though we had been in the center of the fighting for Adelsdorf, the bakery—and the Church remained whole. I was glad for Aunt Agnella—the organ was safe. That night, we had some bread—and jelly, and I shared some of my precious chocolate, having found that eating small bites helped it stay down. The rest I hid.

———

CHAPTER TWENTY-SEVEN

No News is Good News

GEORGE, THE BUS driver was sitting at his usual seat at mother's bakery. His next bus run downtown wasn't for thirty minutes. He wasn't looking forward to the trip even though he had considered himself lucky to finally gain his commercial driver's license, having held one other qualifying certificate when he had tried his hand at being a stock broker. As a matter of fact, he thought he hadn't had much *good* luck in his life, but that changed when mother had become interested in him. Today had been an exception; it had been raining hard all that morning and he was suffering from a heavy spring cold. Worse, his recent attempts to charm the lady had gone unrequited. He knew she was still married, officially, but he had high hopes for their future together. Her financial worries and her lingering grief over my absence had made her increasingly depressed—that and the small amount of customers.

He stared at her and sighed. The years had been particularly hard on her looks. She was getting heavy frown lines across her brow. He couldn't remember any time lately that she had laughed at his jokes.

He got up to use the pay phone in the corner and called-in "sick." Then he approached the counter.

"We're getting out of here," he insisted. "Let's go get a drink."

He couldn't have been more surprised—or pleased. She took her apron off.

Gunda's neighbor opened her door to stop the incessant knocking.

"Telegram, for Mrs. M. Rebhan," the young man intoned. She had no answer. "Can you accept this for her?" He was wearing a uniform with a black bow tie that made him look even younger, and a cap with a Western Union logo on it. He couldn't have been more than fifteen years old.

It was 1945 after all. Next to seeing a policeman at one's door, there was no worse happenstance. Hundreds of thousands of messages had been delivered to loved ones by Western Union Telegraph Company. Most telegrams were not congratulatory, rather they announced the President's regrets as Commander-in-Chief for having to inform the recipients of the death or missing in action notice within. Mother's neighbor didn't even want to touch the yellow envelope.

"She's at her business."

While he was grateful to get the information, the young man wasn't thrilled to hear he would have to reroute this one. On the other hand, someone else could take a turn at watching the addressee collapse—he hated his job for that—and these days, it wasn't as though he could look forward to a tip.

☆ ☆ ☆

The baker looked past the customer he had in front of him. "I'm from Western Union," the woman explained. *She* was wearing a man's cap with a bill. There was writing on her hat that announced she *was* with Western Union. "Is there a Mrs. *M.* Rebhan here?"

"No. She left for the day."

"Well, can you take this for her?" he said silently cursed the rain.

"No!" The baker was firm. "I don't want it! Take it away, take it away!" He came out from behind the counter, gesturing for the woman to get out. For emphasis, he made some poor joke about her being the telegram *boy*.

"The real men are away fighting for us," the messenger scolded. "In case you don't know it, there's a war going on!" She wanted to add that her own husband had been in the veteran's hospital for a year recovering from his wounds, but she didn't have the heart to remind herself how hard her life would have been without this job. She didn't hear the apology.

She would have to call in and re-route the message again, back to the recipient's home address.

✧ ✧ ✧

Needing to stop for the rain to let up, Mama and George had gone for drinks at a local bar. Mindful of the costs of single drinks, they left to buy two bottles of scotch whiskey at a liquor store on the way to her apartment on Clay Avenue. Each of them carried a brown paper bag with one bottle in it. They were equally "under the weather." Full of more than a few shots of liquor, her date was the more melancholy of the two. Having lost his own wife to a long illness, and witnessing the war-time grief in those along his route, he still found it hard to believe that Mama had endured the four past years with no news of my whereabouts; whether I were dead or alive. When they stepped into the elevator to go up to her apartment, he literally bumped into the telegram boy who was coming down.

"Say," the kid asked, "any chance that you know a Mrs. *M*. Rebhan?" He was slapping the telegram against his hand.

Her senses somewhat dulled by her afternoon of measured forgetting, Mama had to think for a minute. She was, after all, still married to *Martin* Rebhan, and without making much more of it, she gave her date the bag she had been holding and reached for the clip board with a blank for her signature.

George held up his free hand. "No, wait a minute." His senses weren't *that* dull. He recognized the yellow envelope; the carrier of so much unwanted news. He didn't want my mother to know the pain it might hold, not after all these years. He turned and said to the messenger, "Give it to me." He handed her both bags of liquor.

"No. Mrs. Rebhan has to sign!" The messenger was adamant. "Is that you?" he asked.

"Yes, I'll do it." She handed the bags back, took the boy's pencil and signed her name, "Mrs. *M.* Rebhan." She immediately had a change of heart. She wasn't so far gone that she could actually *open* the envelope. She took the bags back, and said to her companion, "You read it to me."

It was the last thing he wanted to do, but having made such a mess of his attempt at bravado, he was her hapless servant in this. He peeled back the flap and gingerly inched the folded piece of paper out of its place. He scanned the first set of tapes pasted directly on the sheet. "*The government of the United States of America...*" He began to sway.

His hands dropped to his side, limp and lifeless except for the grip he held on the paper. He was the quietest he had ever been in her company. Moving forward, he put his hands on her shoulders.

"It's not about Martin, Gunda. It's about Sylvia."

She could barely whisper. "Sylvia, my little Sylvia?"

"Yes," he said, his voice rising.

"Is she alive?" She chose what she *wanted* to hear.
"Yes."

Mama began to rock back and forth with him.

He went on. "It says, 'having been found by members of the United States Army near Adelsdorf, Germany...'"

"Let me see, let me see!" she was screaming. Reaching for the message, she dropped both bags onto the elevator floor, smashing the contents to smithereens. The elevator car was immediately filled with the odor of Jack Daniel's and the sound of my mother shouting at the top of her lungs. "Say it again, say it again. She's ALIVE!"

Gunda had snatched the paper and was reading it over. "She's alive!"

It didn't take a minute for George to wish she hadn't dropped *both* bottles. Their feet were awash.

"It doesn't say when she's coming home." Gunda lamented.

That part was going to take much longer.

———

CHAPTER TWENTY-EIGHT

The Beginning of the End

HITLER WAS DEAD. On or about April 30, 1945, the BBC announced his demise. It was over for the European Axis. The radio had come up from the cistern to stay and was full of the fall of the Italians, and the coming together of American and Russian troops. Most of my Adelsdorf neighbors were not so sure how they felt until they saw a strange collection of soldiers on horseback.

I saw a dozen Russian, Mongolian horsemen. They looked more Chinese than Russian to me, but then I had a limited experience with the lady on the train. I learned that these weren't regular army. This Russian presence was more like visiting tourists. They wore long leather coats that were lined with wool and split to cover their legs on each side of their mounts. Their hats were tri-corner throw-backs to the days of Genghis Kahn, although I don't really remember having seen pictures of that army in my school books. Russian troops had been accused of many atrocities—unfortunately, so had been some of the Americans. I had seen some of the "work" of forward troops who had tied a few German husbands to trees while they did, I was told, what they "wanted" with their wives. For the most part, German civilians had not attacked those first Americans when they pushed east. But there were other stories, later proved true, of German women and children shooting at American soldiers. They persevered, acting as snipers and fighting to the bitter end.

Many American soldiers hadn't made it to Adelsdorf. But others had come after my friends with their tanks. They were part of a different group whose job it was to manage prisoners' camps being built in the area beyond the Convent and across from my former school house. I felt it might be a good idea to go there.

I had walked to the convent first, and stopped to see my aunt. There was little Agnella knew that could add to my recent experiences. She and the other Sisters had moved down into a series of cellar rooms under the convent, praying to a variety of saints and ancients "in charge" of impossible causes. They surfaced after both the German and Americans had passed them by on their way east. Agnella hadn't heard some of the radio updates but listened with some relief in learning that Americans were well on their way to Austria. The "good" nuns were happy to have Allied troops between them and the Russians. I thought it best not to mention the Mongolians. I kept many of my thoughts to myself. It wouldn't do to speak my mind about lost German causes.

Agnella was very direct with me. "Look, there is still no government in place, no electricity, no mail, no trains, no newspapers with the exception of a few hand printed flyers circulated by a variety of underground movements. It would be wise," she added, "to sit tight and maintain silence. There are bound to be repercussions. You never know where people stand," Agnella cautioned. I was not dissuaded.

✻ ✻ ✻

The camp was being built in much the same way as Agnella's causeway—sort of thrown together. I watched it growing from holding pens, bare tree trunks turned into posts jammed deep into holes and strung with wire to enclose fields of German soldiers who were just sitting on the ground. The men looked tired to me. Beyond the fields were some long buildings, which it seemed could never be big enough to house all the prisoners that kept being added to the population. There was a gate big enough to let trucks come and go, and a kind of make-shift shack that served as a place for the American officers to meet. What impressed me the most was the energy level among the Americans—and their highly polished shoes. I could tell the officers' rank by comparing their shoe shines with others wearing boots. When we heard of the German surrender, I introduced myself to the really glossy pair seated behind a desk made of planking. He knew who I was.

"You're famous, you know? Our celebrity. What can we do for you today, little lady?" He was tall and clean shaven, a kind of big-brother type with an easy smile. His manner reminded me of my cousin Werner—and I wondered if *he* was still alive.

So much of my halting English came from some hard-to-reach part of my brain. Actually, there were things I had learned to say in English classes at the Gymnasiums. I did my best to ask when I might get back home to America. Once again, I heard that I was going to have to stay in place. First, there would have to be all the German reactions to the official surrender, and then the administrative activity in the United States. No one could promise anything, but I went often to visit.

A few weeks later on my way past the convent, Agnella stopped me in the road.

"We need you to ask the Americans to help us. One of our kindergarten children is very ill—beyond our nursing. Can you go back and see if your officers could get the child to a doctor, or a hospital. Can you do that?"

✿ ✿ ✿

There had been much discussion among the Americans. None of it centered on *if* they could help, just *how* they could. I was so proud of them.

"Nothing much available in Bamberg," said one.

"I agree," said another. "Nuremberg still has a hospital up and running; German doctors available to civilians."

In a matter of minutes a field phone call brought a pair of soldiers to the office door. One was driving an unusual vehicle with open sides.

My open mouth stirred the driver to say, "This here's a 'Jeep,' Honey, the latest version of a Cadillac made in the U.S. of A. Hop in." I pulled myself up with the help of his passenger, a soldier carrying a rifle.

"Now, where's the patient?"

Sister Agnella was standing where I had left her in the road, but she had Sister Anna with her. She held a tiny child wrapped tightly in a blanket.

"OK," said the driver, "you ladies can squeeze in the back."

Agnella asked me to translate for her. She wouldn't be going, just Sister Anna and the child. I let her know that we were going all the way to Nuremberg.

The message given, the tires spun and we burst forward. What a sight we must have been racing down what was left of the highway, the soldiers, a skinny child and a nun with her cowl and the edge of her cape flowing out behind her. Hours later, our precious cargo delivered, we shared some hospital food and watched the soldiers eat ready-made cold rations from cans before we rode back to Adelsdorf in the failing summer light. I was in no hurry to get back. This time I noticed what was along the roadside. Most of the outskirts of Nuremberg were reduced to heaps of bricks and broken stones, so few left whole or unscarred. I was sorry I had wished the tanks on my school. If that Gymnasium was still in one piece, I would have been surprised.

Mama felt as though she were serving out a prison sentence with no hope of parole. This next period in time was going to be excruciating. She had gone back to the bakery with a handmade sign with bold letters announcing that I had been found, alive! She had wanted to take down the jar, but her neighbors insisted on cramming in more change in celebration. In a short time, half of the customers heard about my being alive..

"This is such wonderful news for all of us,"

"Congratulations!"

"So exciting!"

"Mazeltov."

"You can use the money as a college fund," a regular said pushing in a dollar bill. "She'll need it."

By the end of the week, the jar-money fund and the ever faithful butcher's fund reached into the thousands. It remained untouched in anticipation of my future repatriation needs. None of it was used when Mother sold the business six months later to buy a bakery without lunch services. Her new business would require less work, concentrate on baked goods, and be closer to her home address on Clay Avenue. There, she felt she might need to be more accessible for further news of my return.

She had other concerns. She had heard from my father. The lawyer was enthusiastic. "Well, well, my dear, now you have knowledge that can be used on your behalf. We won't have to wait years to have him declared dead. You can have your freedom by divorcing him now that we know where to serve the papers."

It was, at the very least a solution she could work on, immediately.

———

CHAPTER TWENTY-NINE

Once more, again

EARLY ONE MORNING, I had waited for a pause in my conversation with Sister Agnella. I always stopped on what seemed to be a daily walk from Adelsdorf to Aisch. In a moment of reverie, I had asked to be excused to treat myself to a walk through the halls and rooms of the convent. Everything looked—smaller. I caught sight of a few nuns sitting on beds in one of the larger bedrooms and wondered if the Hitler babies had survived. There was talk on the radio of the plans to divide oversight of Berlin among the British, the Americans—and the Russians. With regard to Agnella's other suggestions for discretion, I kept this news and my questions to myself. In the room, one of the older sisters looked up. I thought she might have been my catechism teacher. There was a moment when I thought of running in to celebrate the nun's survival, as well has my own, but the room had gone quiet. I supposed by then that everyone had heard of my tank ride—or maybe learned that my name was, Sylvia, and not Betty after all!

I moved on down the hall and went into a room still reserved for Kindergarten. I smiled to myself when I spied the wooden blocks and tea sets nestled near the wicker carriage I had been given for that birthday in the fall of 1939. I caught my reflection in the long windows looking out at the big elm tree where my party had been held. I was taller, my face longer with higher cheek bones and full lips. I came to the conclusion that like me, the wicker carriage was in pretty good shape for its age. Stepping through the side door, I went out to the area where I had celebrated my first birthday with the nuns. Was it possible? In four months I would be thirteen?

The alarm intruded. The clanging bell was being rung at high speed. Standing under the tree, I was joined by nuns spilling out of the convent. They were chattering like magpies having seen the intruder in the fields adjacent to the grounds. Wandering through knee-high mist rising from his steps was a man in a German military coat gone ragged and torn in a variety of places. If he hadn't been staggering forward, he could have been taken for a scarecrow. The covey of nuns had poured through the door behind me. One was carrying a broom, another, a kindling hatchet from the kitchen. They were shooing the man as they would crows from rows of corn, trying to convince him with a series of chirping commands to turn back into the fields. In spite of their warnings, I moved forward with the boldest of defenders. I heard a livid Agnella behind me.

"Sylvia, Sylvia, you come back here!"

The man was some twenty paces away, his face covered with hair and a large coat remnant that had been wrapped around his head to cover his ears. He sank to his knees, groaning more that using his speech. "Sylvia, is it you?"

I knew him!

"It's all right," I called back to the astonished nuns. "It's all right. It's my Uncle Walter!"

I couldn't believe that he would live another moment, even as the nuns clustered around him and began to minister to him. Great clouds of dust and mist swirled around their long skirts. And there was so much blood. His feet were bleeding, oozing more crimson than I had seen in the entire mayhem surrounding me for all those years.

Agnella seemed dumbstruck. It was so unlike her.

Another nun barked a command. "Child, go get your Aunt Betty!"

I didn't move. I knew it wasn't the right thing to do—yet.

"Go, child. You have to get her before this man dies!"

Walter fainted.

Agnella looked at me and finally understood. She spoke for both of us, for all of us, really. "Stay where you are, Sylvia. Sisters, let us get our patient out of the damp and treat his wounds. You must trust me in this. Sylvia knows. If his wife sees him like this, she will have a heart attack and both their deaths will be on our souls."

We carried him into the main hall, putting him on a straw mattress pulled from a bed and placed on the floor beneath him. We peeled layers of cloth and filth from his entire body. Agnella assigned me to hold his hand and made others, disregarding all protests by the squeamish, to stoke the fire in the main hall fireplace and burn every scrap of cloth they took from his head and the bits of leather, paper and cloth that had covered his bloody feet. I joined them in picking lice nits from the part in his hair.

There were moments he seemed to regain some level of consciousness, and then he lapsed into a kind of delirium. "I have to keep going," he moaned, "… must keep on walking."

"Rest," Agnella implored, "just close your eyes and rest. You are safe; you are home." He believed her.

The nuns washed him like a baby, a cloth discretely covering his body while they scrubbed his head with a brown soapy mixture that they used on his hands and arms. They poured water over the dirty foam and let it drip into a basin. He was patted dry. From some resource they produced a balm to cover the serious holes in his feet. Nail scissors were produced to clip back the hair that had folded over his lips, and balm was applied to the tip of his nose and his seriously cracked lips. Water was trickled into his mouth, and some thin soup was brought into the room and dropped on his tongue. Someone was at his side all day and into the night. Two nuns and I watched over him until he fell into a deep sleep.

Early in the new morning, I felt him squeeze my hand and ask, "Betty and the children? Are they here with you?"

"No, Uncle." He struggled to raise himself. "But," I added quickly, "they are all well...and safe in Adelsdorf."

He smiled and winced when several of the cracks in his lips protested. "Can you bring your Aunt Betty to me?"

I wanted to tell him about everything...about the tanks, but I knew better. What he needed was my aunt, so I went for her. I pedaled at a good rate, not especially fast. I wanted to think about his return, what I would tell Betty, how she might react. I climbed the stairs quietly. She was asleep between Horst and Ingeborg. They looked positively angelic and I stroked her arm gently until she stirred. Before she could speak and ruin the moment, I told her about Walter—my way.

"A miracle has happened at the convent. God has returned Uncle Walter to us... to you and the children. He has some injuries, so he needs you to come to him."

She sat up asking me, "Is this true? My Walter?" She eased herself out from between the children. "Walter…at the convent?"

"He has walked a long way. His feet are really bad, but he's alive."

"I must go to him. Can you stay with the children?"

God bless her! And He must have; she was _calm_. She stopped to use the chamber pot and then to brush her hair, not complaining to her reflection in the tiny piece of mirror that had survived the battles. She smoothed on her remaining dress and began to change her appearance from the inside out. I could actually see her loosen the tightness around her mouth. I watched years drift away as she said his name over and over.

"Take my bike," I called after her. I watched her from the bottom of the stairs. She ran along side and then hopped on the seat, coasting and shortening the distance; her legs were much too long to actually pedal from a sitting position, so she stood up. I was never more proud of her or happier with her reaction. I went back up and slid between the two children, hoping they would let me stay there for another hour or two before I would walk them over to see their father. I wondered if they would recognize him. He'd been gone for over two years.

It was well after two o'clock in the afternoon when I
arrived with the children. Betty had not moved from
her place next to her husband. The children were very
shy with their father but Horst had been intrigued
with all his bandages. Ingeborg sat on her mother's
lap and sucked her thumb. No one disturbed them
until supper time. Several nuns took the children
down the hall to play with the Kindergarten toys. It
wasn't until afternoon the next day when Walter had
managed to share his inner-most fears and actions
as an American member of the German Army. He
held forth in several sessions with his wife and his
"nurses."

Walter's stories were eventually told in a series of
visits. Cautious of the sensibilities of his audience,
he told what he could share without fear of reprisal.
Betty's version considered her need to believe he was
a non-combatant:

At the rank of an enlisted soldier, Walter had
learned to carry and shoot a rifle, but was soon used
as clerk by his German officers. His many skills and
his keen mind kept him off the field of battle—and
fairly well fed. He was billeted in decent quarters
and counted himself luckier than most service men.
Older than most of the conscripts, they had little in
common. And as a family man, he had been incredibly lonely.

Never told exactly where he had been sent, he
believed he had become part of a last ditch attempt to
shore up holes in the eastern front—well beyond the

Austrian border, perhaps somewhere in Russia. He
had been away less than three months when the mail
stopped. It was his first bit of evidence supporting a
dim view of the outcome of the war. In spite of what
he was told about priorities, he knew; if they couldn't
move the mail, they couldn't supply troops. He tried
to ingratiate himself with his superiors, essentially
to be privy to maps of the area.

Office machinery and its repair became his
number one priority. To insure his assignment, he
became expert in fixing typewriters, phones and
teletypes. He was equally good at dismantling a
perfectly good machine so that he might be assigned
to repair it, a subterfuge he had long suspected in
factory workers years before. His explanation was
to condemn perfectly good equipment as having been
made by non-German workers, certainly a possibility
having witnessed the use of slave labor. The officers
believed him. His main job was to survive and return
to his family, a cause made equally frustrating by not
knowing exactly where they were, either.

He told Betty that he was counting on two military tactics to save his life, long enough for him to
be captured alive—the Germans were retreating,
pulling back into Austria, and the Allies were driving
east. He believed that most of the men in his outfit
had discussed their preference to surrender to the
Americans. The most difficult attitude to shake was
his own growing paranoia based on his experiences.
He feared most, being turned in as a traitor and

could not share his thoughts with anyone. Isolated in every possible way, he waited for a rescue that would include not getting shot by three sets of ideologies, the advancing Russian, the Americans, and his own men whom he became convinced would sacrifice him as not "really" a German. He waited.

What Walter told Agnella was mindful of *her* roots:

Their headquarters having been over run by Americans, his superior officer, hoping to gain favor, volunteered Walter as an interpreter. He remained loyal to this and other German Officers in his unit until it was announced that at the end of April, Hitler had died in Berlin, and finally, that the German surrender had been unconditional. Walter had then presented himself to a colonel in the American division and told them his predicament. He had been an American citizen, pressed into service by a hostile situation. As a clerk, he had never fired a gun and was not responsible for a single American fatality. He told them about his wife, his two children, and then he told them about me. The American Colonel said he would have to wait for his story to be verified, and that might take months. At the end of his strength, Walter agreed to make no trouble, to be of service to the Americans with the recognition that he would receive no pay, but he would be fed and have a place to sleep until his "mess," like many others could be cleared up. He waited some more.

Later, one of his versions included the growing understanding that he would have to convince the Americans of his loyalty; he considered some of his casual interchanges with the enlisted ranks. One evening, while sharing a cup of real coffee, he overheard a soldier talking about New York and what he missed most about America—baseball. Walter mentioned the bakery, the Polo Grounds and what he knew about the Giants. Cautious to a fault, he acknowledged that it might have been a mistake to do so.

"Oh God," he admitted. "If you are a Dodger or Yankee fan, I'm done." The private laughed and couldn't wait to tell his platoon leader. "Walter's an American all right. Who else would dare to tell a New Yorker that he should be afraid to know anything about the Giants?"

For once, Walter was going to get home before the paperwork was finished.

What surely happened—for everyone's ears, never changed much in the telling. Walter said. "I didn't get sent to the prison camp. Not only did they let me go, they gave me a captured German motorcycle, which, by the way, they taught me to drive. They managed a ten-gallon can of gasoline, a compass, food, some money and maps. The Officer and I discussed the dangers of going before everything was settled and order restored, but I told him that I couldn't wait any longer. I would have had to try to escape otherwise, and take my chances. I had to find out if my family was still alive. I rode at night, wearing my German uniform coat and cap, and I carried a pass to use if I got stopped by any Americans. I tried to sleep during the day. There had to be several repairs to the machine, but I was able to see to those. I did my best to seek out some gasoline, but truly, I had nothing left to trade for it. After a while, there simply wasn't any to be had, anywhere. I had hundreds of miles to go when the gasoline ran out. I traded the motorcycle for food and began to walk. My boots, well they held up until the mountains. I tied the soles on with strips of my coat. When I crossed the border into Bavaria, I headed for Aisch thinking that Agnella would know about my family...and you my dear Sisters. If you hadn't been here..."

Everyone agreed. Whichever version, Walter's survival and his return to his family, THAT had to have been a miracle.

—

CHAPTER THIRTY

Going West

WALTER'S CONDITION IMPROVED dramatically. Surrounded by his wife and children, he couldn't help but mend. Of all of my activities, he showed the most interest in my connection with the American officers at the camp. When he could bear to put on socks and an old pair of soft leather boots, he asked me to take him out there.

"Can you introduce me to your officers?"

"You want *me* to introduce *you*?"

"Yes, you are our leader in this. I have a proposal I want to discuss with them, a way to get you nearer to home."

I knew then that my Uncle Walter had returned for more than one reason. I was a part of his family business. He meant to take care of me.

"I want to get the Americans to agree to let us all go back to the Rhineland—to our old neighborhood—my family. I can take much better care of you all there. And it is time for us to get away from here."

He had an idea that such a departure could be accomplished. He would take his band of refugees—and lead us back before the authorities were overwhelmed by the hundreds of thousands of displaced persons wanting to go home. It was a well-considered solution. The officers agreed. While the Americans were busy with particulars, Walter struck up conversations with some of the prisoners who were anxious to hear news of their own. He understood fully. He spoke about his plans to take his family west as soon as possible. Having consulted those in charge, he received permission to return one afternoon with bits of paper and some pencils and promised to deliver news and notes for a variety of prisoners who had provided addresses in the Rhineland. Finally, with passes signed by the Americans, he was ready to work out a way for us to travel.

With my Uncle Walter reassuming his role as head of the family, I was brought around to the idea that I was going to get home. And his family—Betty and the children, they could be together in a home of their own. He managed to convince what he called *my* Americans to provide a variety of permission slips. I think he had become good at talking to the military. With a series of precious passes, we would use the only working transportation available—the rails.

✶ ✶ ✶

Picking through a pathetic pile of clothing and items that had survived our nomadic life, Uncle Walter, Aunt Betty and I began once again to pack for the road. On this trip, our suitcases were three large burlap sacks, one of which Walter had stacked full with letters from the prisoners of war. We set off on foot for the train tracks outside Adelsdorf, alternating carrying our *luggage* and the two children. Horst proved to be a sturdy walker, but Ingeborg was less willing to plod along beside us. She was carried. We were all encouraged to keep up, but Walter set a pace that was considerably slower in deference to his feet, which were still mending.

I really had no idea what our accommodations would be, but I was still surprised when the first train finally came to a halt in response to a signal from a railroad worker. Behind the engine was a huge open car full to the brim with coal, pitch black coal. There was nothing else for us to do but help one another climb up the ladder at the end of the coal car, having heaved the sacks up ahead of us. Betty climbed first. Horst followed close on her heels, and I on his. I pushed my head under his bottom and with Uncle Walter close behind carrying Ingeborg, we pulled and shoved our way up onto the rough surface of the fuel briquettes. They were sharp and slippery at the surface, and shifted under pressure. We dragged ourselves into the middle, away from either side and rearranged the sacks as our surface for sitting without genuine pain. We did our best to "dig in" to maintain our balance and keep the two children from toppling forward or backwards. Once the train picked up speed, we had to hunch over and hold to each other on to avoid the rush of air bouncing us off into the countryside.

After a few miles, I was able to reach up and wipe the tears from the corner of my eyes. I wasn't crying. It was the beginning of what would be a life-long tear production in reaction to wind blowing over my face. Horst used the occasion to laugh.

"You have two big black eyes," he giggled.

It wasn't long before I countered with a remark about his new black mustache. He had tried to wipe his dripping nose with a hand that had examined several pieces of coal. Uncle Walter too had wiped some sweat from his brow, altering his hair line. Only Aunt Betty had managed to keep her hands off her face.

"I have to go pee," Horst complained. His problem was easily solved as his father gripped his waist and we all watched him make a commendable arc out into the wind and then the fields beside the tracks. We were discrete when Walter followed suit, but Betty and I would have a harder time relieving ourselves. I was the first volunteer, of course. Dropping my drawers in motion was the least of my problems. Betty had suggested a way for me to turn around while she held my wrists in those firm hands of hers, and I squatted over the edge, allowing my business to drop into the passing grasses. Walter returned the favor for his wife. In spite of all she did to balance her larger frame, when finished, she stumbled forward and fell across the coal. Hauling herself back onto the burlap, she was filthier than all of us put together. No one laughed. Soon enough, we wouldn't care or comment on what we looked like. We were more than ready to get off when we were told.

The next leg was accomplished on a train that had fewer surfaces where we could sit. An engine pulled a series of flat cars on which there were several airplanes, their wings folded and tied down beside the recognizable fuselages of small American fighter planes. Walter showed our passes to a surprised engineer.

"Well, I have no reason to doubt all this, but you'll be my only passengers. You might want to squeeze yourselves up on the flats between the wheels and hang onto the blocks and chains holding down the landing gears."

I don't know what that man thought about the five blackened people who stood looking up at him, but since we had been alone on the coal car; we hadn't had any expectations of company. Certainly, these smooth units would be more dangerous than the grooves we had been able to scoop out for safety among the pieces of coal. Between the planes, we had to hang on to one another in shifts, ever aware of the danger of sliding off. Walter held Horst between his legs, Betty gripped Ingeborg in a similar way, and I nestled between them. We had to remain vigilant and AWAKE.

The next train had a series of box cars with sides and doors. Elated by the prospect of sitting or lying down on a surface in such a car—we considered it an incredible piece of luck. Our sacks were tossed into the cavern opened by Walter and a trainman. Betty, the children and I allowed ourselves to be pushed directly by hands on our bottoms up into the dark. We fell asleep in the few seconds it took Walter to pull himself in.

Walter was our mainstay, our father, uncle and captain. Using his American Army compass, and one of his precious maps, he managed to plan access to a series of trains that were at least moving in a mostly north-westerly direction. We had little packages of bread and cheese. On one occasion a trainman provided water from a pail. Sometime we had a two mile trip north followed by a train dipping to the south. Other routes backtracked east before crisscrossing a piece of track headed for the Rhineland. Having filled our nostrils with the rarified air of potential, our troupe was ready for the last of its challenges. The train approached a water tower near a road.

"This is as close as we will get on a train," he announced. We climbed down.

Uncle Walter had his crew sit by the side of the pavement until, after a full night of scanning the roadway, he flagged down a truck. Aunt Betty did her best to brush us off. She needn't have bothered. We climbed into the back of a vehicle that had certainly transported some animal or other. From my farm experience, I offered, "Pigs. There have definitely been pigs in here." Aunt Betty wasn't impressed, but Horst wanted to know what they must have looked like.

✷ ✷ ✷

The street was empty. I had lost track of time in the truck, but when we got out, it couldn't have been more than just an hour or so before dawn. The sun hadn't risen.

"Just a bit more," Walter urged us on. "We are at the eastern end of Tönisheide."

It might have been two or more miles before I noticed anything other than the road in front of me. In several lots there were neat piles of stones that looked as though they had been purposely piled in rows according to their size; next to them, a collection of broken window frames and blackened cement. At a distance there were several empty spaces where houses had once been. I don't know if I was the first one to spot it when we turned the corner. There was Werner's apartment house, still standing tall. I didn't dare to look across the street.

"Oh Walter," Betty had said with the first bit of excitement she had allowed herself in days. "Our house; there's our house."

It was true! The entire block stood just as it was when we left it. Nothing, it seemed, had flattened or splattered it, or even damaged the street pavement itself. We were falling behind Betty who had once again showed a remarkable capacity to move when she wanted to. We all broke into *her* trot.

☼ ☼ ☼

"Who the hell are you?" a man asked when Walter opened the front door leading into the kitchen. All those years, Betty had held onto the apartment key. There was a group of three sitting at the kitchen table.

"I am the legal tenant," said Walter in a matter of fact and very clear tone. "We are back from the east and are reclaiming our apartment."

Faced with four filthy vagabonds hauling equally black sacks, the squatters couldn't protest if they wanted to. And so it was that without complaint, and in less than a day, they gathered what belonged to them, moved out and we moved back in.

We camped for the night on Werner's living room floor; later, the family and I had gone across the street and taken up residence. Evidently, Walter had known what he was talking about; the law supported such activity as it went on all the time in areas where citizens had been bombed out and moved into quarters that weren't. But I think we must have left a huge black spot on my aunt's living room carpet.

Once again, I took up the space next to the window in our old bed, the mattress having been worn in totally different grooves. I did my best to sleep as long as I could without rolling into a much larger Horst. Ingeborg barely fit lengthwise in the crib but none of us, as I recollect had any trouble sleeping for hours on end. I think we cleaned up sometime in the middle of our dreams.

———

CHAPTER THIRTY-ONE

The Wheels Grind

MY MOTHER HAD her lawyer *hound* Congressmen, several other lawyers and a slew of Red Cross workers and war relief members. They had worked tirelessly to meet the situation and find the appropriate way to amend it. Following every suggestion, she had written copious letters trying her best to get proper documentation. The problem of course became a bureaucratic one; I would need a passport. The Chief of the passport division in the Municipal Court of the City of New York wrote to Mama and included a letter from New York's Congressman Quinn. Until the American government had established embassies and or a diplomatic or consular officer in my German district, none could be issued. The benefits were the certifiable facts that mother was indeed a citizen, as was her daughter, and the maddening eventuality; the problems would be solved. On September 25, 1945,

I spent my 13th birthday in Töinesheide. It would be eight more months before any return could take place.

When Betty found out that the Velbert Gymnasium would be holding fall classes, she insisted that I reenter. In some ways, it was as though I had never left. She insisted on braiding my hair first thing in the morning and sent me off. Some of my friends were still there on my first day back, and the teachers, having spent but a few minutes testing me, insisted that I gather up a new set of books and get to work. It was surreal.

By late November in 1945, I was immersed in studying geometry and science. No one even suggested history or geography for the moment. Everyone there had to sign up for English, though. I was often amazed by all that I had learned of that language.

More waiting, waiting...no one was more surprised than I when I found I would be spending another Christmas in Germany. The bright spot in such a scenario, I had grown so much, that like it or not, Betty was going to have to contact the local seamstress and have some clothes made for me. Certainly, there was no local shopping. The women who still had an operating sewing machine and some aunt or uncle's leftover dresses or suits were making a living cutting down these ancient wardrobes and making dresses, skirts or jackets to fit their smaller clients.

Already wearing an undergarment, a type of vest to flatten my growing figure, I managed to eat enough to bring on my menses. I became a woman. In a mystical way that I never could explain, having shared this news with my girlfriends, at the same time, so did they. Perhaps we all knew psychologically that it was safe to become females.

I caught the eye of a passing service man. Sergeant Ronald Nutiari said he was taken in by my sad face. One cold January day, he saw me sitting on the curb. He had passed by more than once without striking up a conversation. "You have such sad, mature eyes in that young face," he said to me that morning." An Englishman attached to the British Army of the Rhine, he worked in a field office in the area; he literally walked by my home every morning on his way to work.

"I say, are those new roller skates on your feet?" he asked. "Why aren't you up rolling around?"

"I got them for Christmas. I *have* been skating," I responded to his particular and peculiar way of asking a question in English. "I'm just sitting here thinking."

"And what could be so important that it would keep you from skating about this morning?" He seemed genuinely interested.

"I was thinking about my mother." I said in careful English.

"Truly?" He was cautious. There had been so many casualties. I don't think he really wanted to know if my mother had been one. He asked, "What is it you were thinking?" He settled on an age-old mother-daughter relationship and offered, "Have you had a tiff? A disagreement?"

"Oh no, not anything like that. I can't argue with her," I explained. She's not even here."

"Where is she, then?" I think he was so glad he didn't offer a standard solution that would have included Heaven or some such spiritual location.

"She's in America."

"That's so?" He was genuinely relieved and then surprised. "Well then, what are you doing here?"

"I've been here, well not exactly...*here*...the whole time. I didn't want to say too much. "I was in Bavaria for a while."

He was intrigued. He looked at his watch not daring to be late for duty but wanting to hear more. "What happened?"

"The war," I said, "the war happened."

"And then?"

"And then I couldn't go."

"Go where?"

"Home."

"Home?"

"Yes, to America."

"Is that what you want to do?"

"Oh yes. I want to go home to my mother."

"And that would be...where?"

"New York City."

He was caught up in the possibilities. "And why haven't you gone back there now that the war is over?"

"I think I have to wait until my mother comes to get me," I said with some uncertainty. "But I don't even know if she knows I am here...in Tönisheide."

"Well then, you must tell her, mustn't you?" He sat next to me on the curb.

"I haven't been able to," I explained as though I were speaking to a child instead of being one. "There still is no mail service."

"Ah," he said standing with a firmness that meant he'd made a decision. "I can include a letter to her when I write to my family through the company mail. They could forward it from London. Would you like me to do that?"

"Could you?" I was on my feet. The suddenness made me start to roll backwards, and I had to grab onto his arm.

"Brace up," he steadied me. "I can jolly well do that for you, Miss." He reached into his pocket and drew out a piece of paper and his pen. "So, now where can this American mother of yours be reached?"

"1109 Clay Avenue, the Bronx, New York City, USA."

He wrote it down. "Tell me, what shall I say?"

"Can you write that I am well, that I am *here*—and I want to go *there*?"

"I'll do my best," he was in earnest although he wasn't sure what difference it might make my legal status until I said, "I'm an American, too. I was born there...and I still have my certificate."

He seemed relieved. "Ah, then, we shall write to your mother and tell her to hurry along and fetch you back, shall we?"

"Promise?" I dared to ask.

"On my oath!" He had another idea. "When I come by tomorrow, you should have a note ready for me. I will include it, mail it to my mother, and have her forward it to yours. What do you say?"

"Mama, oh Mama!"

✡ ✡ ✡

Early in May of 1946, the letter was in Mama's apartment mailbox. The tissue-thin blue envelope had an overseas postmark and she knew it was important. She read Ronald's short letter first. It had been dated December 30, just before New Year's Eve. She considered it the best late Christmas present she had ever been given.

"...The enclosed letter from your daughter was handed to me to forward. Although I don't know your daughter...I have seen her often and can say she looks very fit and cheerful." He cautioned that Gunda wouldn't be able to respond to the military address on the envelope as he was being released from the British army "in a month's time" but hoped that she would be "reconciled with your loved one very soon."

My mother took heart, she finally knew *exactly* where I was. She called the lawyer. When he answered, she screamed, "I know where she is!"

He didn't need to ask who was calling.

Uncle Walter had been very supportive. He had inquired locally from Ronald's British Office. He too, found that an American passport and transportation would depend on the arrival of an American government representative. He promised me to find a way to deal with any message he received from the American Consul's concerning the issuance of a passport.

Easter had come and gone.

I had a new, (it-had-been-someone-else's cut-down dress) for the Holiday procession—there's a picture of me...and I even had the attention of a young boy. Looking back, I can honestly say that this beginning, an awareness of feelings beyond hunger and survival almost weakened my desire to go home. It had been a year since my American soldiers had rescued me from that brewery cellar outside Adelsdorf. I had to stiffen my resolve. I filled up my autograph book with messages of good will from my newer friends at school and the neighborhood. They were still signing into May, and then June. I tried to remain confident— there were very few free pages left.

✠ ✠ ✠

Uncle Walter's life and his family's future were not problem-free, either. In any case, he had to be content with some of *his* good fortune. He was alive, once again he had a job, and unlike the more than millions of military and civilians who lost their lives, his family was safe and sheltered in familiar surroundings.

His problems concerned what he knew about my father. Walter had always known more about Martin—who had since been released from military service—than he could share with his wife, and certainly more than he was ever willing to tell me. The men had never been "that friendly" before the war. What he thought of Martin's politics...dangerous ground. He was never sure who Martin's knew. There were going to be serious repercussions and certainly he didn't want to endanger his family, nor me by association. He also concluded that the dissolution of the Rebhan marriage was none of his business. How and why Martin left my mother to return to his country of birth, what Walter had learned about certain decisions, all these and their attendant politics would have to be reconsidered later. His immediate concern was the degree of involvement he should ask my father to take as far as I was concerned. He had promised my mother to return me, and that is what he meant to do. Mindful of his promise, albeit way overdue, Walter considered the timing and the effort it would take to get me north to a port of embarkation when the Americans could arrange it. Like it or not, the plans might have to involve my father.

Late in the spring, at the end of my school term, the long-awaited message arrived. The government of the United States was prepared to issue me a passport. Further, a place had been reserved on a Liberty ship that would sail from Bremerhaven in July, and summarily return one Betty Sophia (Sylvia) Rebhan, citizen of the United States of America, to my homeland—and to my mother.

Walter had thought it through. He told my father that he should prepare to take me to the coast. There was no protest. Walter and Aunt Betty gathered the contents of a small suitcase for my trip. What my Aunt Betty thought, well that was not one of Uncle Walter's considerations, nor, did he really ask that she share *his* sense of loss. I believe I had become more his daughter than Martin's, even as I had never really been Betty's. Walter kept his thoughts to himself but would have grieved more had he not been sure of the rightness of getting me back to my *real* mother. So much of what transpired among us was more difficult than dodging falling bombs. I wasn't sure how much was my youthful resistance; But I never really felt part of Betty's family. Through all of it, I never stopped believing that I was part of my Mother's.

I took what would be my last look at what had been my German residence. I would have few nostalgic feelings for the house I had lived in for so many years. It was soon to be part of my past, a period I would have to put away if I had any hope of living happily in America. I kissed Horst and Ingeborg, sorry to leave their little round faces. I wondered how they might do without a big "sister" to plead their cases with their mother. Perhaps, too, I was young enough to be sorry to leave my roller skates.

✳ ✳ ✳

Evidently, my father might have thought he could gain favor with my mother. She did have to answer a government inquiry about her relationship with him. She was candid but assured those who wanted to know, that she would NEVER consider remarriage. Whatever he knew about the possibility of his returning to the United States, he did show up at the Rhineland apartment in plenty of time to take me to the port.

He was attentive. I think he showed me more affection than I had had from him in all those years that went before. I couldn't help but realize that even though he was my father, he wasn't my "Papa." I barely knew him. I still didn't know then about the money he took when he left my mother, no one discussed his support of the Nazi party, his reasons for joining the German army—nothing of that nature. I was prepared to accept him at his word when he said he wished me a safe journey. He did also ask me to give his greetings to my mother and strange as that seemed, I said I would. Eventually, I would come to avoid him.

I had come full circle at last. The irony of sailing back from the port of Bremerhaven, the ocean liner's namesake, was lost on me until much later. Instead, walking across the pier in the *port* sent memories of New York City floating in my mind. I caught myself remembering and looking around for red caps and their luggage carriers—and my doll buggy. Can you imagine? Instead, soldiers by the hundreds were hauling their sea bags over shoulders already burdened by back packs, many containing souvenirs as well as socks, raising their weight well beyond the suggested limits. I had no trouble carrying my suitcase. My precious items were my paperwork and the well-worn leather autograph book I had managed to hold on to since I had sailed away from my mother in 1939. Like me, it was seven—almost eight years older. Inside the front cover was a faded picture of "Little Sylvia" sitting at my parents' feet. Before I left, someone had used white paint and covered over my father's greeting to Hitler.

Once again I set out to cross the Atlantic. This time I waved goodbye to my father as he stood alone on the pier below me.

———

CHAPTER THIRTY-TWO

"Rub a Dub, Dub"

THE MARINE FLASHER was a "tub." America's President Roosevelt had commissioned a series of ships that even he called, "Ugly ducklings." Certainly, in a sea of swans, it was a stubby collection of two oil burning boilers, a reciprocating steam engine and a "bucket of bolts." Based on a British design, it was unlike the Cunard's Queens, Mary and Elizabeth that had also been pressed into service as troop carriers. The Flasher, like her sister ships had been mass-produced to "get the goods" overseas. These "Liberty" ships had done yeoman service plying the Atlantic and Pacific Oceans bringing supplies to the European Allies who were fighting Germany and Italy, and the Pacific theater combatants, island hopping on their way to conquer Japan. All in all, more than 700 of these USS (United States' Steam Ships) had been sunk. After May 8, 1945, the formal surrender of Germany, the end of the war in the Pacific, those ships that survived and remained seaworthy were dispatched to bring the boys home—and me.

The Flasher was to sail in July of 1946 from Bremerhaven to New York. With its crew, it would carry 900 war-weary members of the armed services and the first set of civilians, 100 American citizens like me that had been detained in some manner. My number, 64, indicated that on that trip, only 36 other civilians had been kept apart from their stateside families longer than I had.

Close to 441 feet long and 56 feet wide, the Flasher was not the smoothest of sailors. Most of her anxious passengers learned quickly to settle themselves up-wind of the bridge side vents, which soon spewed forth the foulest of air reflecting the state of oceanic activity. There was a series of storms that threatened to wash away the superstructure, keeping us passengers off the main deck, the one place we might have recovered from the smell of engines and illness. Soldiers and civilians suffered beyond motion sickness. Those who weren't sick to begin with, soon reacted to the wretched noises and smells of those who were. Many had grown weak from lack of nutriments and sleep.

I really don't know why, but even on the worst of days during the more than 14 required for crossing, I was not sick. While others hung over the side, green and dehydrated, I stood at the high table provided for our meals and let the crew bring me anything they had to offer. I had my pick of coca-cola, fruit I hadn't seen in years, and ice cream. I ate everything, and like a good convent-bred girl, I cleaned my plate. After a week, the crew members knew enough to bring me the best, first. I was never sorry or critical of my accommodations. I slept in a tower of bunks that reminded me of shelves. I was only sorry that it seemed to take so long.

The Marine Flasher, meant to be an efficient hauling vessel, could do about 11 knots, not even half of the forward motion plowed by the Bremen years before. I stared at the water in spite of my acceptance of the idea that it would be weeks before I saw land again.

From that very first speck of dark on the horizon, the call of "land ho" was more difficult to bear than all the time at sea. It took forever to scan the shoreline for the mouth of the harbor past the "lump of land" that was Ft. Hamilton in Brooklyn. It was at least another day before the waters of the Lower Bay slapped against the side of the Flasher's hull. I did my best to maintain my position. There were so few openings at the rail; but even I had to sit on my haunches pulling my feet under me to avoid being stepped on. I stood at last for the Statue of Liberty. We slid past her feet, we were that close. A great noise went up among the men. It was more than shouting. There were whistles, and a pounding of feet on the deck— and hands thumping the rails. Tug boats spouting water came along side. It was still hours before our floating bathtub inched into a northernmost pier alongside the city spires that I remembered from my youthful ferry boat rides to Staten Island. I joined the chorus of happy home-comers singing out names.

"That's the Chrysler Building!"

"Hey, the Empire State!"

"Isn't that the Roosevelt Hotel?"

And beyond—the arches of the George Washington Bridge. We were traveling up the west side of Manhattan Island. For a moment I thought we were going to sail under the bridge and go up the Hudson River. The tug boat pushed the stern sideways, and the back swung around pointing the ship straight into the finger-like docks of pier 90 covered with people, packed together waving handkerchiefs and miniature American flags.

I looked down into all those faces and wondered if my mother was among them—and if she were there, would she recognize me?

My mother had needed to go to the bathroom. She had stood there for hours, not daring to leave her spot at the forward edge of the crowd on the pier—it was filling along with her bladder.

"We're meeting our son," said a woman behind her. "We saw you here when we first came." She leaned forward and whispered in Gunda's ear. "I have to go, do you? My husband doesn't want to leave this spot, and he won't let me go alone."

Mother turned to look. She judged them to be in their late forties, but thought she could no longer really assess anyone's age. She knew the war had added years to all those who had served the war effort by waiting for the return of those they loved.

"Save our places," she told the man in a voice that offered no choice in the matter. Mother grabbed the woman's hand, and together they pushed their way back through the crowd.

"We are here for our son," the woman said again as they snaked back from the bathroom. "He's been wounded, but it's just his arm. He said to look for his cast, that it would make him stand out. Who are you waiting for?"

"My daughter."

"Oh, will she be in uniform? Was she a nurse? How will you pick her out of all those faces?"

"No, she wasn't a soldier or a nurse. I'll find her. I'll find her, you'll see. She'll be easy to spot."

"Oh, was she wounded too?"

"No, but even you will be able to see her in that crowd. She'll be the only child."

———

CHAPTER THIRTY-THREE

Finis

"SYLVIA!"

Mama had seen me coming down the gangplank.

"Sylvia!, Sylvia, Sylvia!" I could hear my name. And then, "It's your Mother, your Mutti. Here, over here." She was jumping up and down so fast her voice broke. "Syl—vi—a!"

I scanned the crowd more than once to find the source of that voice. It seemed to be coming from an area off to my right, but the woman who was bouncing into view had blondish hair and wore big, round horn-rimmed glasses. I can't remember any rush of emotion. I just know that it was a good thing she had found *me*. I never would have recognized her. I stood in front of her with my seven years of memories crammed into that little cardboard suitcase and looked as hard as I could to resurrect the face I had said goodbye to on the deck of that other ship so many years before.

243

"Snukie," she said. "Don't you know me? It's your mother?"

She pulled me so close; she forced the breath I had been holding out onto the front of her dress.

"Don't cry," my mother rubbed the space on my back, between my shoulder blades. "Don't cry."

I hadn't been crying, it was that eyes tearing-in-the-wind thing…but I knew enough not to disappoint her. I said nothing, really, I just let her talk.

✡ ✡ ✡

We began to snake through the remains of the crowd, passing the couple alternating hugs with their son, his cast and arm sling held gingerly above his head.

"This is my daughter, Sylvia," Mother said with mounting pride and conviction. "She's home, now, she's finally home." Those who could took notice as she led me away from the edge of the wharf, back toward the ladies' room. She held my hand and her forearm in an intense grip.

"Do you have to tinkle?"

I smiled. It was so *motherly*, this business of *going* before leaving.

Of all the images I could have conjured up, I remembered this particular one. My mother used to make fun of my fierceness about public bathrooms. There had been that time I had to go in the middle of the Shirley Temple movie and I thought the bathroom was dirty. She hurried me along while other mothers were covering toilet seats with tissues.

She was still hurrying me. "Come along now." I had to practically drag her to a sink to wash my hands. She resumed her introductions to several sets of families enjoying their reunions, leading me beyond the cement dock to the street. There were miles of Checker taxi cabs lining the curbsides.

"You look beautiful, my dearest, beautiful. Just as I thought you would." Mother spouted her stream of words along the sidewalk, finally pouring us into a yellow cab.

"This is my darling daughter, Sylvia," she announced to the driver. "She came back to me today—from the war."

The cab driver pushed his flag over to start the meter. "Glad to meetcha" he responded. "Come on that ship, didja?"

I nodded. My mother was still talking. I did my best to pick out some of the things she was sharing even as the cabbie said. "Where're we goin', Honey? Home, is it?"

"No," my mother countered. "Drive us across the bridge to New Jersey. I am taking my daughter to the Palisades Amusement Park"

The cab driver was pleased enough. Some of the gas restrictions had been lifted and he envisioned a good fare and generous tip.

"You'll love this park," she went on, scarcely drawing a breath as she squeezed me, hard.

✧ ✧ ✧

You know those geese that get fed more than they need—to make wurst out of their livers? It was like that—my mother's welcome. She covered everything—seven years of life on the home front; her decision to let me go with Aunt Betty and Walter, why she'd settled on Agnella and the convent—all while the cab sped along Riverside Drive. By the time we got to the toll booth for the bridge, she had peppered her word stream with the bakery news, and my father's disappearance with the money; she tossed everything in with her bouquet of changing addresses—old and new. And somewhere between one side of the bridge and the edge of the Palisades, she threw in getting divorced and her intention to marry one of the "bus drivers, George." Then there was his son, and the revelation that my ready-made new family would have a brother in it. I strained to think of her...to call her Mutti, or even Mama as she was buying tickets beneath a huge wooden roller coaster when she turned and became serious enough for her voice to crack.

"I worried; I worried all the time you were gone. I was so afraid!"

And she told me about the MovieTone News even as we were in a small booth taking our pictures, which came out all done in a strip from a slot on the outside of it. She took off her glasses for those shots, and looked more like the mother I remembered.

We went on a swing ride that went round and round a big pole until our seats hung out sideward on their chains. That was a big mistake. Mother got sick right there in front of crowds of people, and I thought, *I've come all this way and she's going to die in front of me, in New Jersey.*

Of course she didn't, and she rose from the grassy spot where she had rested next to the sidewalk after I had given her the ice a woman offered me from her drink.

And I ate a cone that looked like a waffle and held the ice cream roll on its side after I took the paper off it. And she talked some more.

And I listened. I tried so hard to concentrate as she spoke a mixture of English and German, switching back and forth when I raised my eyebrows as a kind of word filter. She told me where we were going to live, where we would be spending the summer, where she thought I would learn better English, and where I would go to high school. And she told me about the jar, the one constant, the jar of money and the butchers' contributions that had started out for my return and ended up as a fund for my college.

"I never touched a single dollar." She told me. "It's there for you, for your schooling."

I was sucking in air to feed her frenzy of words. I hadn't said two of them.

At the end of the day, we retrieved my suitcase from a bank of lockers I found intriguing. She had put money in a slot in a door and taken out the key she used to open it later.

I'm sure I finally spoke up to ask for another ice cream, and we sat on a bench while I ate it from a "Dixie" cup, a container I remembered from the Marine Flasher. It had one of those round lids with a picture of a movie star or a battleship printed on the inside, under a piece of tissue paper you had to lick before you peeled it back to get a good look at the image. I ate it with a flat wooden spoon and focused on my mother as she tried to account for my lost childhood.

As I recall, on that homecoming day, I shared very little of my stay in Germany. It was easy to remain silent while I was eating, and I knew that I wouldn't be able to convince my dear Mama that I had come to process so much more than she could imagine. She so wanted to explain that it wasn't her fault. It wasn't Uncle Walter's or Aunt Betty's. None of it had been any one person's "fault." I had left her as a child, a huge WAR had taken place and I had come home mature in ways she would never know. Oh, I had always been aware of her capacity for hard work; knew she would try to make up for it all by reintroducing me to the "land of plenty," but nothing she could ever do or say would raise my sense of wonder any higher than it had been. The war, the ever pressing needs of the war, and the convent, the bombings, the cellars, the White Russian, the train strafings, ghosts on the farm, my mad dash on the bike, my rescue by the tank soldiers, and Uncle Walter's miraculous return. How could she possibly compete? I accepted it on that day. I would never be able to make her understand.

The war hadn't been the only thing that had taken my childhood from her—and from me. Yes, it had been fraught with dangers, but I never fully absorbed nor "saw" many of them; frankly, I skipped over the worst of times, played a detached kind of hide and seek, closing myself off just to get by.

I know now that some of my childhood experiences couldn't be compared to those suffered by the adults who were fully aware and lived through a different kind of deprivation. For so many years, I wasn't really *thinking*. In every sense of the word, I had been a child. I knew that, but, it had been also been a noisy, incredibly active time for me, a series of challenges played out in an otherwise mindless game of survival.

I sat there, eating my ice cream and looking at my mother. In two months I would be 14. How could I feel so numb, when for years away from her I had ached so much for her to be the one to put me to bed, to read me stories, to speak in her soft tones? It was a puzzlement, believe me. I know I didn't slide over on that bench to have my body touch my mother's because I regretted my past. No, I reconnected with her on that day because I knew Mama would be part of my *future*—at last!

"Snukie" my mother had asked, squeezing me tight. "Aren't you glad to be home? Wasn't this the *most* exciting day?"

I looked out across the Hudson River, took in a huge breath of New Jersey/New York air, and hugging her I spoke. "Of course I am. Of course *it* was," I said with conviction. And truly, for that moment, we both needed to believe I meant every word.

———

And Now?

WHERE'S SYLVIA? SYLVIA married and had two children, Ralph and Wendy. Her husband, Ralph died in 1984. She is the grandmother of two boys, Sam and Curtis, and a girl, Samantha. An enthusiastic hiker, she has survived three strokes which resulted in her having been airlifted out of the Grand Canyon and the southern Arizona mountains by helicopter and a canyon exit on a mule.

Gunda died in New Jersey after all, but not until 1991.

Martin petitioned to the United States government and in spite of his politics was given permission to reenter. He remarried several times and died in the early 1960's.

Uncle Walter reentered the United States and became a citizen again. He carried on his work as a tool and die maker. He died in 1993.

Aunt Betty reentered with Walter and lived with Horst until she died in 1996.

Cousin Horst entered the United States with his parents and became an American citizen, married and had one son. After his father's death, he took care of his mother until she died. He died in 2002.

Cousin Ingeborg: The one family member who died an untimely death. She succumbed to a massive infection following the rupture of her appendix and died in Germany at the age of twelve.

Aunt Agnella remained a member of her order and died in Aisch, Germany in the late 1970's.

Cousin Werner moved to the United States and married and remarried. He still lives in New Jersey.

About the Author:

LINDA LAMURA MCFADDEN was born and raised in Brooklyn, New York. A graduate of Packer Collegiate Institute and St. John's University, in her long career as a writer and editor, she has written with a by-line for a variety of eastern and western newspapers and was writer/editor for Al-Anon Family Groups. Her credits include an eclectic array of work as editorial consultant for the Associate Producer of the CBS TV film; Under the Influence; editor of the prize winning hard cover Mountain Images, a Photographic Essay of Eastern Appalachia; and the creator and script writer for an interactive video game. She is the mother of seven children and grandmother of 19. For over ten years she was a Writing instructor and member of the Adjunct Faculty of Pima Community College, and a certified substitute in the Catalina Foothills District in Tucson, Arizona.

NOTES

From the author in the year 2011:

While all events were reported as they occurred, eventually many conversations had to be fleshed out to accommodate what happened and are second or third hand accounts. Names otherwise forgotten were substituted to add to the flow. Outside sources were used to confirm historical events.

They are:

The Bronx: See http://www.aolsve.worldbook. aol.com/wb/Article?id=ar610460&sc=-1; http://ency-clopedia.thefreedictionary.com/

Sylvia's name: Martin's hesitancy may have confused the hospital record keepers, too, as they reported to the city. Sylvia's "official" birth certificate still continues to carry the "wrong name" —Betty Sofia, but her documentation was amended for her adult passport.

Lucky Strike cigarettes initially came in a green and gold packaging with a bull's eye on the front. In 1943, George Washington Hill, President of American Tobacco Company, in response to wartime shortages of chromium and copper used in inks, changed the packaging announcing "Lucky Strike green has gone to war." an ad campaign that was not entirely popular but did increase sales.

http://www.wclynx.com/burntofferings/adsluckystrikegreen.html

World war II was also called "The Second World war," by the Allies.

NY Subways and Elevated trains: See also: h t t p : / / w w w . f o r g o t t e n - n y . c o m / SUBWAYS/9thavel/9Ave.html

The New York Giants: The franchise began with factory owner John B. Day in 1883. The NY Giants played in the Polo Grounds until after the 1957 season when it was moved to San Francisco, California. The NY teams dominated the National League in the 1930's. Many baseball players served in WWII. The teams were so watered down that the Girls' League started to capture fans, but Major League Baseball went on through the war. They participated in:

1933 World Series, beating the Washington Senators four games to one

1936 World Series the Yankees defeated the Giants four games to two

1937 Yankees defeated the Giants four games to one.

1951 the Yankees beat the Giants four games to two.

See also http://www.baseballlibrary.com/ballplayers/N/New_York_Giants.stm

The Polo Grounds: The original facility at 110th Street and Sixth Avenue was followed by the other three at 155th and 8th Avenue having been expanded and altered until 1911. Before hosting the NY Giants, the variety of Polo Grounds housed the NY Metropolitans from 1883-1885; the NY Yankees from 1912 through 1922, the NY Mets from 1962 until 1963. Closed by September 18, 1963 it was demolished April 10, 1964 and the site became the Polo Grounds Houses established by the New York City Housing Authority..

See also: www.ballparksofbaseball.com; and *http://en,wikipedia.org/wiki/Polo Grounds*

Harry Stevens, & Co. Food Service Franchise: *Author's notes: At a luncheon meeting with members of the New York City Housing Authority, which purchased the Polo Ground and its land for a future public housing development, Harry Stevens Jr. shared the story of how he and his college-age brother developed their stadium food business. They told it to Frank

P. LaMura, Chief of the Land Acquisition Division; it was one of my father's favorites, one I heard long before I met Sylvia. As my father was a Real Estate Broker and Appraiser who often was chosen to offer expert testimony in New York City courts, I had no doubt about the story's veracity:

He said the Stevens boys, home from college to attend the World Series in the Polo Grounds, could smell the aroma of fresh bread from a bakery down the street. It gave them the idea to ask their father to support them in a company providing a business that would offer more than peanuts and Cracker Jacks to the Polo Ground spectators. Harry Stevens, Sr. already held several franchises to sell programs and souvenirs in New York ballparks. He funded their idea, and they began selling hot dogs at the Polo Grounds. I should add that my father, however, was a died-in-the wool Brooklyn fan and late in his life published a series of stories about the Dodgers.

–Linda LaMura McFadden:

Cracker Jack: Popcorn and peanuts prepared with a caramel coating and presented in a box. Invented in 1893 by F. W. Rueckheim and Brother, presented at the first Chicago World's Fair. The confection is mentioned in a still popular song by Jack Norworth and Albert von Tilzer and performed at baseball stadiums during a period between the "away" team and the home teams' seventh inning. See: http:www.crackerjack.com/history.php

The Bund: In 1939, many New York City news-papers, The New York Times and the Herald Tribune carried unflattering columns. Their archives can be examined for a variety of editorials and articles and quotes on the matter of the Bund. Also see:

http://www.longwood.K12.NY.us/history/yaphank/ german_American_bund. htm and http://www.ihr. org/hr/v07p419_Peel.html

The Bremen: Back in a berth in Germany, the navy made a decision to use it as a troop carrier. Those plans never came to fruition. The ship became a floating accommodation for German soldiers. In March of 1941, "a deranged" crewmember set the entire ship afire; there was no saving it. It was turned into scrap metal that was sent to Nazi plants making munitions.

Winston Churchill: The elected Prime Minister of the British Isles.

Franklin Delano Roosevelt: The elected President of the United States.

See also: http://www.greatoceanliners.net/ bremen.html

Niederbronner Schwestern: Name of the Roman Catholic religious order of nuns in Aisch, Germany.

Clipper Ships: By 1940, Pan American World Airways operated a fleet of "flying boats" from

LaGuardia Airport in New York City to Lisbon, Portugal. See *http://www.centennialofflight.gov*

Harlem: Among those who later reported on the causes and effects of the altercation was noted author, James Baldwin. Born and raised in Harlem, he had been on his way to his step-father's funeral. His writing had lifted him into the literary world heavily peopled by white writers, but his Harlem childhood made his views particularly relevant. He described what happened culturally in Notes of a Native Son.

See: Baldwin, James. "Notes of a Native Son." 1955. *James Baldwin: Collected Essays*. Ed. Toni Morrison. New York: Library of America, 1998. 63-84.

Negro: An accepted term in the 1940's for "African Americans" and "blacks."

History of Germany:
Gleichschaltung: Total control of Society
http://encyclopedia.thefreedictionary.com/
Germany

Rationing: Government control and allotment of hard to provide goods during war time, *i.e.* gasoline, fats, oils, butter, tin goods, even bread and milk in some countries.

World war II http://www.aolsvcworldbook.aol.com;

Adolf Hitler: Dictator of Germany. See also http://www.historyplace.com/worldwar2/

The Gestapo: Name given German Secret Police force. See: http://www.spartacus.schoolnet.co.uk/GERgestapo.html.

Secret Weapon: German scientists were working on plans for the Atomic Bomb.

See*: http://Gi.grolier.com/wwii/wwii_atom.html*

Battle of the Bulge: A successful German counter attack late in the fighting, from December 16, 1944 to January 25, 1945, given the name by U.S. Forces' journals. See *http://ice.mm.com/user/jpk/battle.htm*

Pope Pius XII: Elected by the College of Cardinals in Rome, March 2, 1939. See: also http://*encyclopedia.thefreedictionary.com*

American soldiers in Adelsdorf: The National Archives at College Park, Maryland maintains supportive journals and map overlays for the 12th Armored Division, its 714th Tank Battalion in particular, with a map and narrative of their operations in Adelsdorf from April 14th through the 16th in 1945, including their stopping to rebuild the bridge at Adelsdorf and their interviews with civilians. They proceeded with their swing to Laningen and beyond where they were temporarily halted by a run-in with a "herd of horses." CCB – Boxes 16204, 16207, CCR- boxes 16208 – 16218; TKBN 23 – boxes 16243-16246; TKBN – 23 boxes 16247-16248; and TKBN – 714 boxes 16249-16250; in particular 612-Tk- (714) -0.7

Western Union®: Preceded by the NY and Mississippi Valley Printing Telegraph Company in 1856, which followed the invention of the telegraph by Samuel Morse, the company no longer sends telegrams. It was a mainstay of wartime messaging but now is known for its capacity for global money transfer services.

See: http://www.westernunion.com/info/

Movie Tone News: A variety of web sites consider the use of newsreels in American movie houses (among others) between features during the war. One of them is: *http:history sandiego.edu/gen/newsreels/*

Movies: Gunda's frequent attendance during her daughter's absence included seeing movies that won Academy Awards. Their history can be reviewed at http://www.filmsite.org/oscars30.html

Notes by German Prisoners of war: Walter personally delivered all messages he had been give when he returned to the Rhineland.

Liberty Ships: While these particular US Steam Ship casualties are mentioned as below 800, the highest rate of casualties of all Allied sea-going supply ships reached over 1,700 sunk, damaged, captured or detained.

See also http://www.angelfirae.com/in/shiphistory/libvicship.html

Palisade's Park (Amusement Center): History, articles and books noting the long-time appeal of this major east coast attraction, see *http://www.palisadespark.com*

Dixie Cups, Ice Cream: From 1930-1954 cup lids had a series of pictures on the bottom side next to the ice cream. See http://www.go-star.com/antiquing/dixiecups.htm

———

Acknowledgements:

THE AUTHOR RECOGNIZES the following for their unparalleled professional and personal assistance:

Sylvia, for her honesty and clarity, especially when forced to rummage through her own ancient archives, some of which were painful as well as exciting.

John J. Peirano and Richard Keilly, Nina Kersels for their insight and support; William and Kay Wehunt, army history; Ann and Bob Schilstra, copyediting; Irene Kyriacos McFadden design; Pat Mahoney, research; Marilyn and Leonard Miller, hospitality, my late sister Gertrude Steinhauser's funding; and my brother Edward LaMura's invaluable baseball notes; Sandra Bruggemann;

And

My children, who have provided funding, transportation, housing, celebrations and love in spite of my failures; Jeffrey, Thomas, Christopher, Susan, Katherine, John and Frank; and their wives, husbands and children, Anne, Denise, Robert, Pamela; Mike, Briana, Kelsey, Sydney, Megan, Peter, Maura, Kerry, Casey, Olivia, Joseph, Christopher, Demi, John, Mike and Luke, Emily, Colleen, Molly, and Franky.

———